THE PULSE

SECRET WAR

Writer: Brian Michael Bendis

Artists: Brent Anderson & Michael Lark

Inker: Stefano Gaudiano (Part 4)

Colorist: Pete Pantazis

Letterer: Virtual Calligraphy's Cory Petit

Cover Art: Mike Mayhew with

Avalon's Andy Troy

Assistant Editors: Nicole Wiley, Molly Lazer

& Stephanie Moore

Editor: Andy Schmidt

The Pulse created by Brian Michael Bendis

Collection Editor: Jennifer Grünwald

Senior Editor: Jeff Youngquist

Director of Sales: David Gabriel

Production: Loretta Krol

Book Designer: Carrie Beadle

Creative Director: Tom Marvelli

Editor in Chief: Joe Quesada

Publisher: Dan Buckley

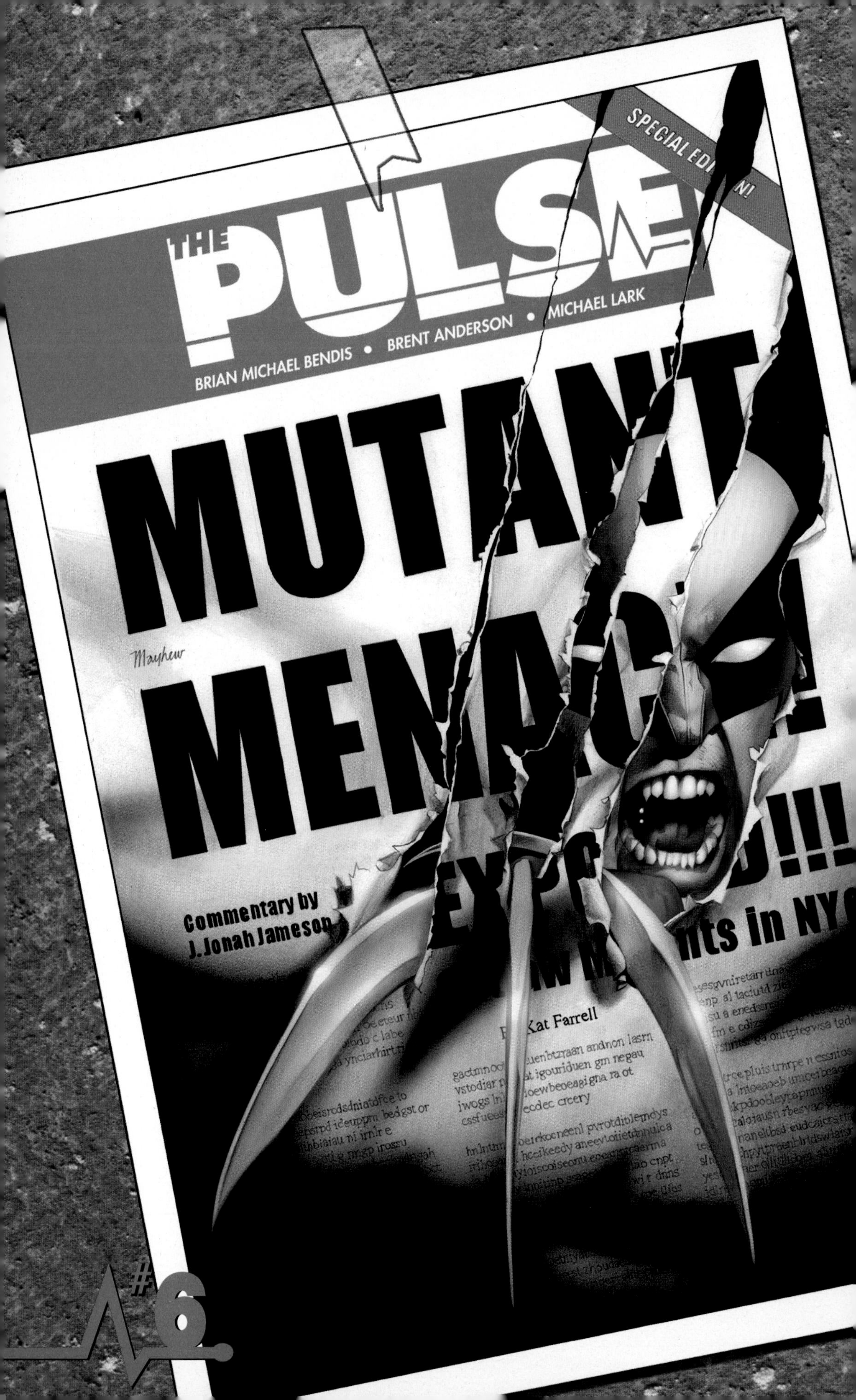

SPECIAL ED
N!
THE PULSE
BRIAN MICHAEL BENDIS • BRENT ANDERSON • MICHAEL LARK
MUTAN
MEN
Mayhew
Commentary by
J. Jonah Jameson
nts in NY
Kat Farrell
#6

The Pulse November 10, 2004, Vol. 1, #6

THE PULSE

Jessica Jones

Ben Urich Staff Writer

Kat Farrell Staff Writer

Jessica Jones Consultant

Luke Cage Hero for Hire

SECRET WAR PART 1

Ben Urich Staff Writer

Jessica Jones, a former costumed super hero, is now the owner and sole employee of Alias Investigations--a small private investigative firm.

Jessica is now pregnant with the baby of her boyfriend Luke Cage, hero for hire.

Jessica has taken a job with the *Daily Bugle* as a super hero analyst. Publisher J. Jonah Jameson has teamed her up with award-winning reporter Ben Urich to help him paint a fair and balanced picture of the world of super heroes.

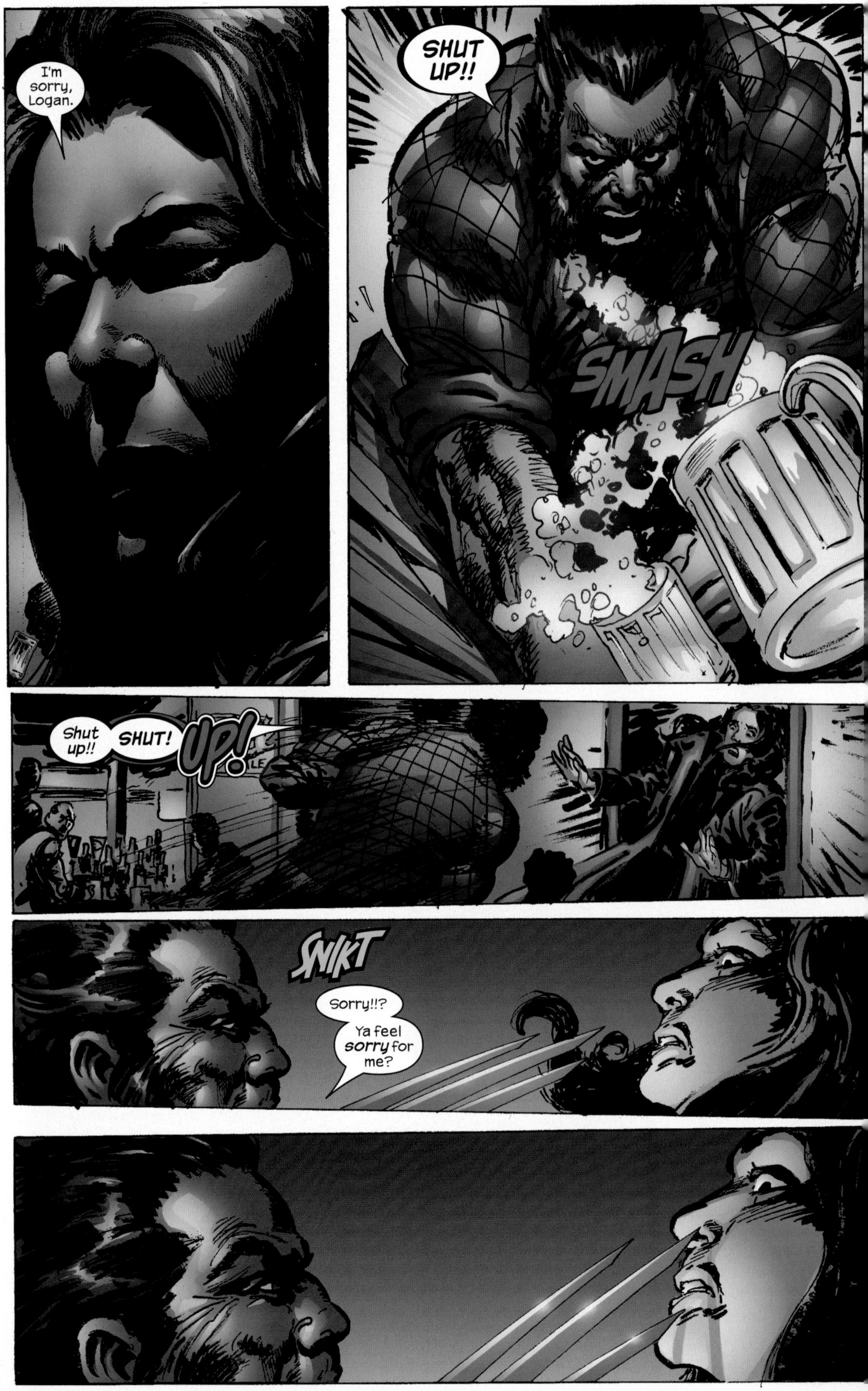
I'm sorry, Logan.
SHUT UP!!
SMASH
Shut up!!
SHUT!
UP!
SNIKT
Sorry!!?
Ya feel sorry for me?

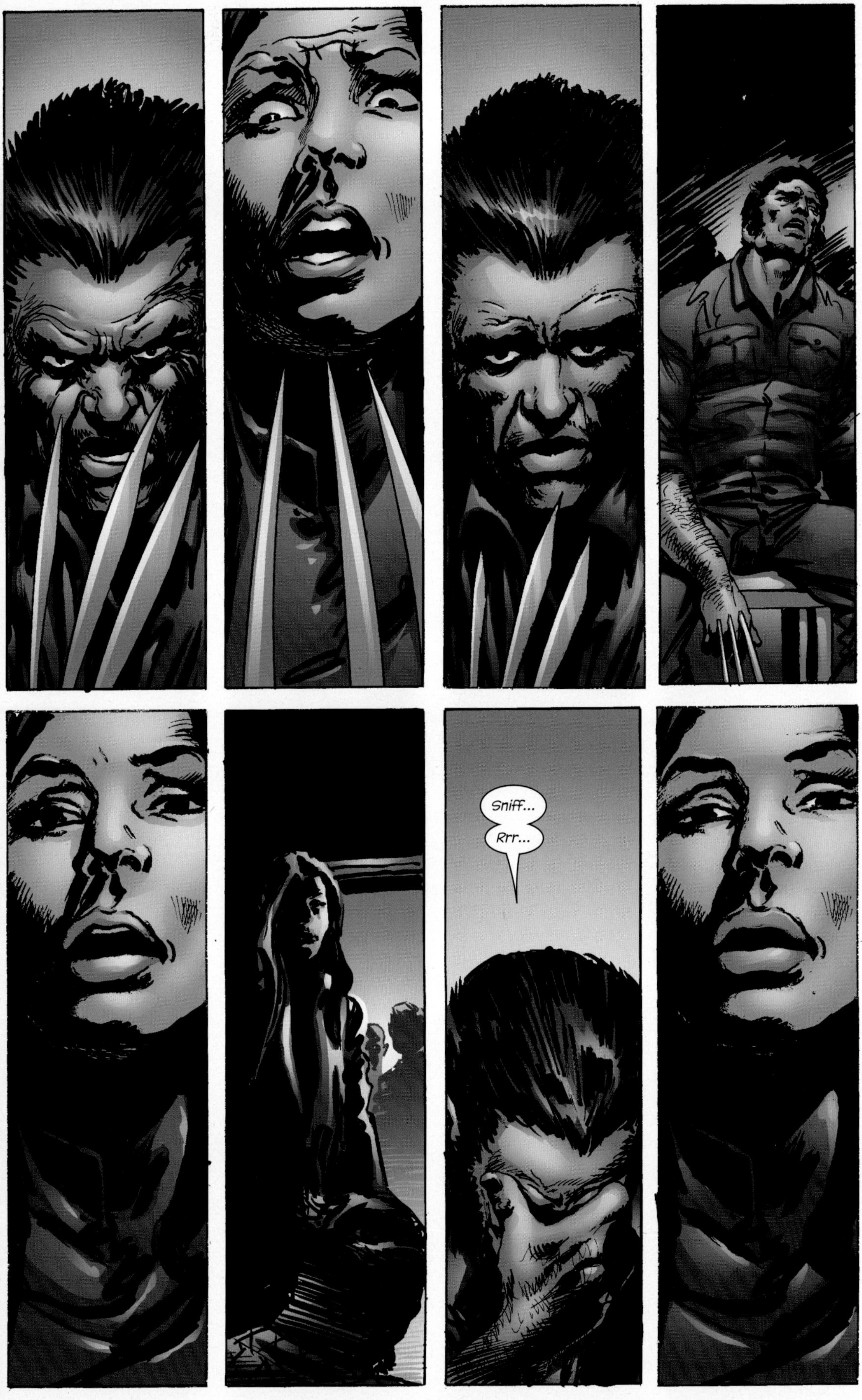
Sniff...
Rrr...

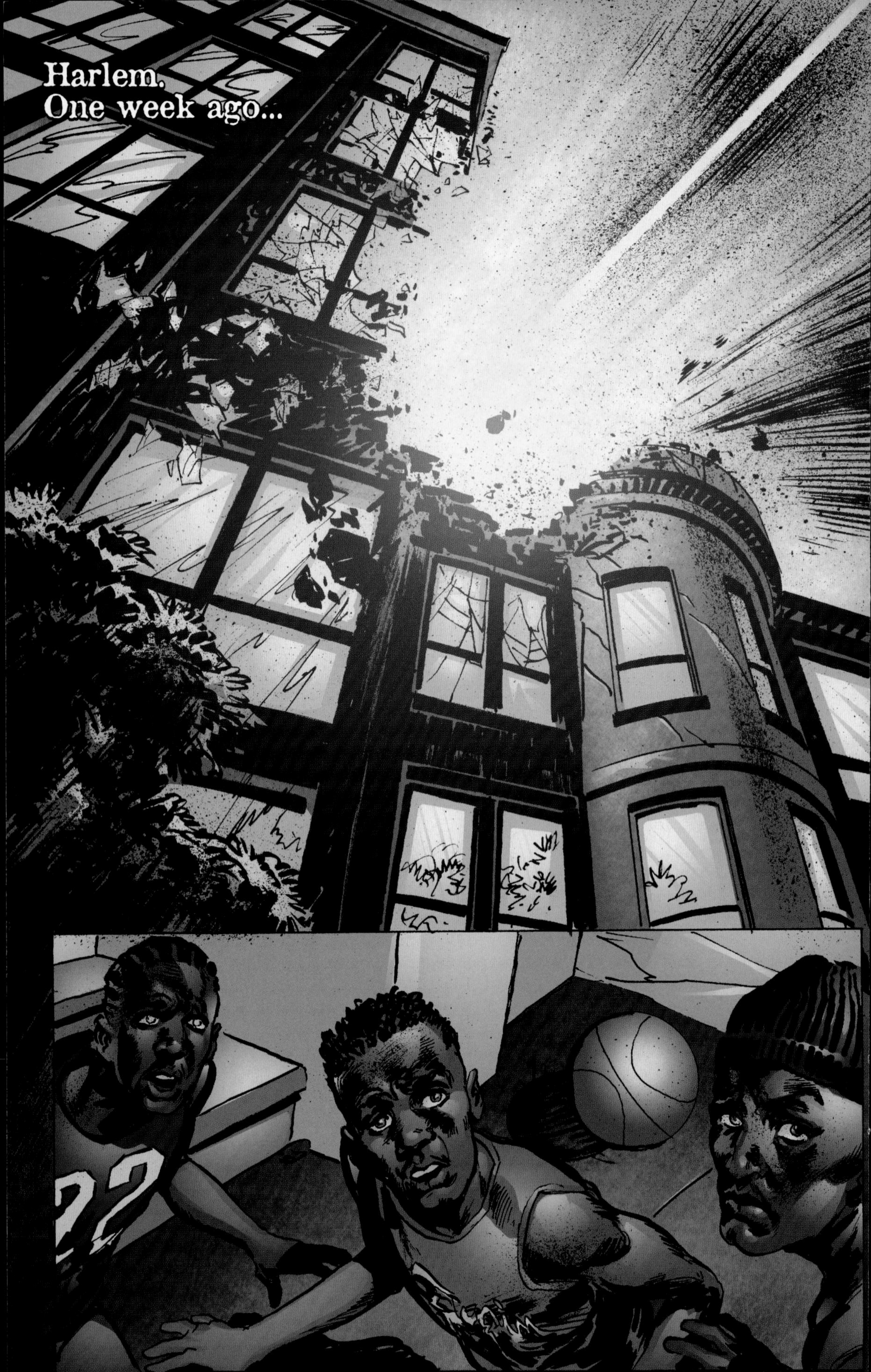
Harlem.
One week ago...

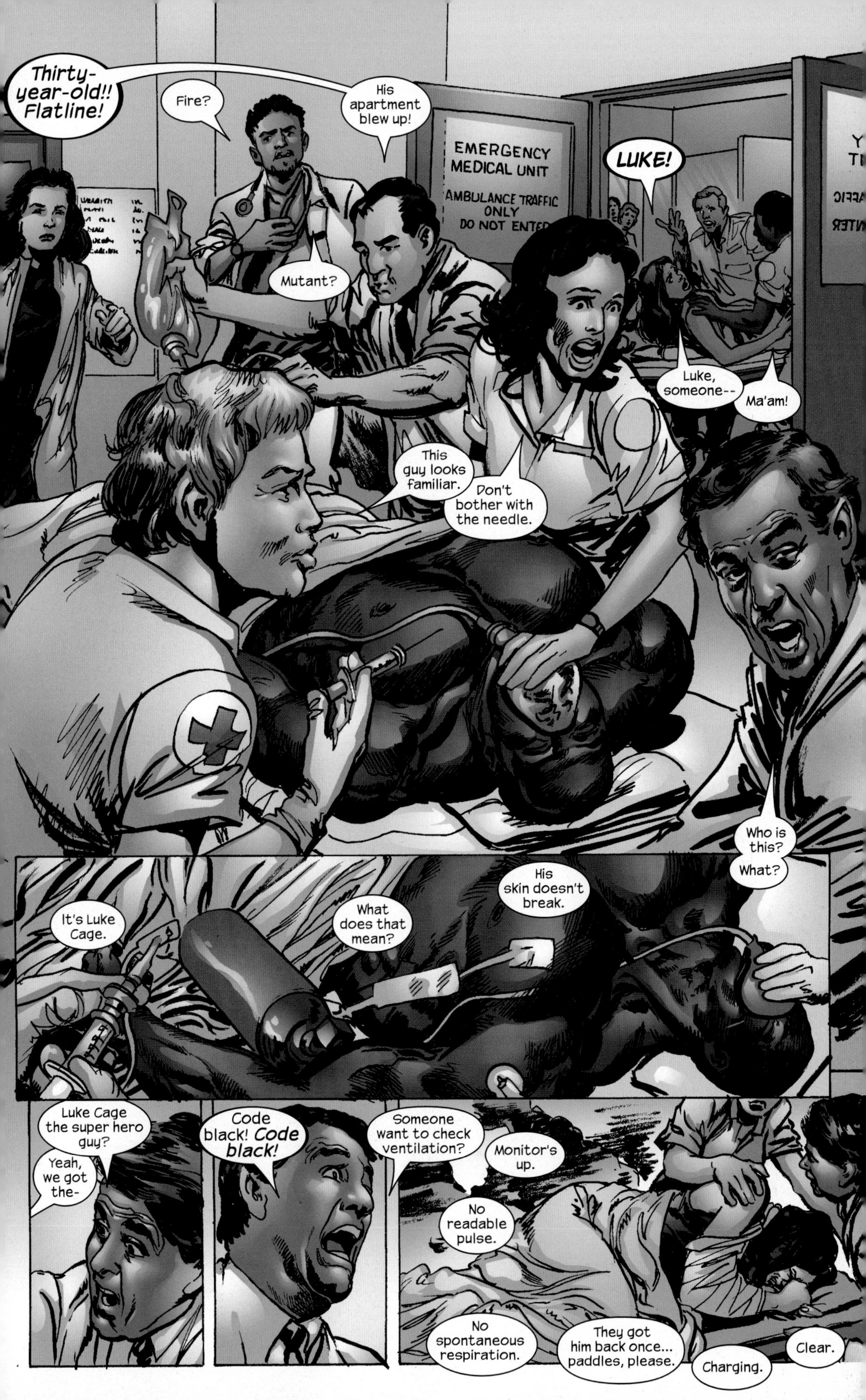
Thirty-year-old!! Flatline!
Fire?
His apartment blew up!
Mutant?
EMERGENCY MEDICAL UNIT
AMBULANCE TRAFFIC ONLY DO NOT ENTER
LUKE!
Luke, someone--
Ma'am!
This guy looks familiar.
Don't bother with the needle.
Who is this?
What?
It's Luke Cage.
What does that mean?
His skin doesn't break.
Luke Cage the super hero guy?
Yeah, we got the-
Code black! Code black!
Someone want to check ventilation?
Monitor's up.
No readable pulse.
No spontaneous respiration.
They got him back once... paddles, please.
Charging.
Clear.

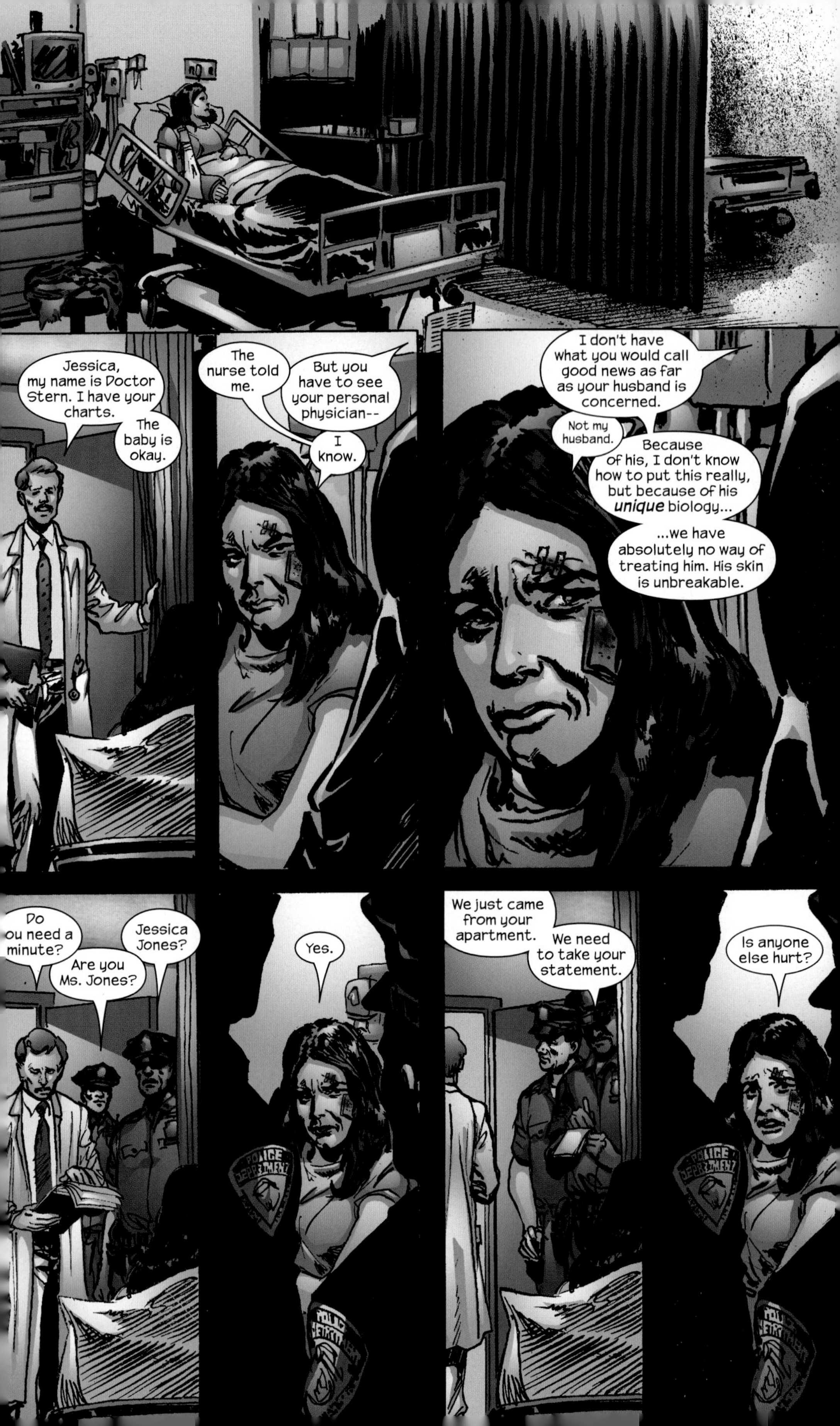
Jessica, my name is Doctor Stern. I have your charts.
The baby is okay.
The nurse told me.
But you have to see your personal physician--
I know.
I don't have what you would call good news as far as your husband is concerned.
Not my husband.
Because of his, I don't know how to put this really, but because of his *unique* biology...
...we have absolutely no way of treating him. His skin is unbreakable.
Do you need a minute?
Jessica Jones?
Are you Ms. Jones?
Yes.
We just came from your apartment.
We need to take your statement.
Is anyone else hurt?

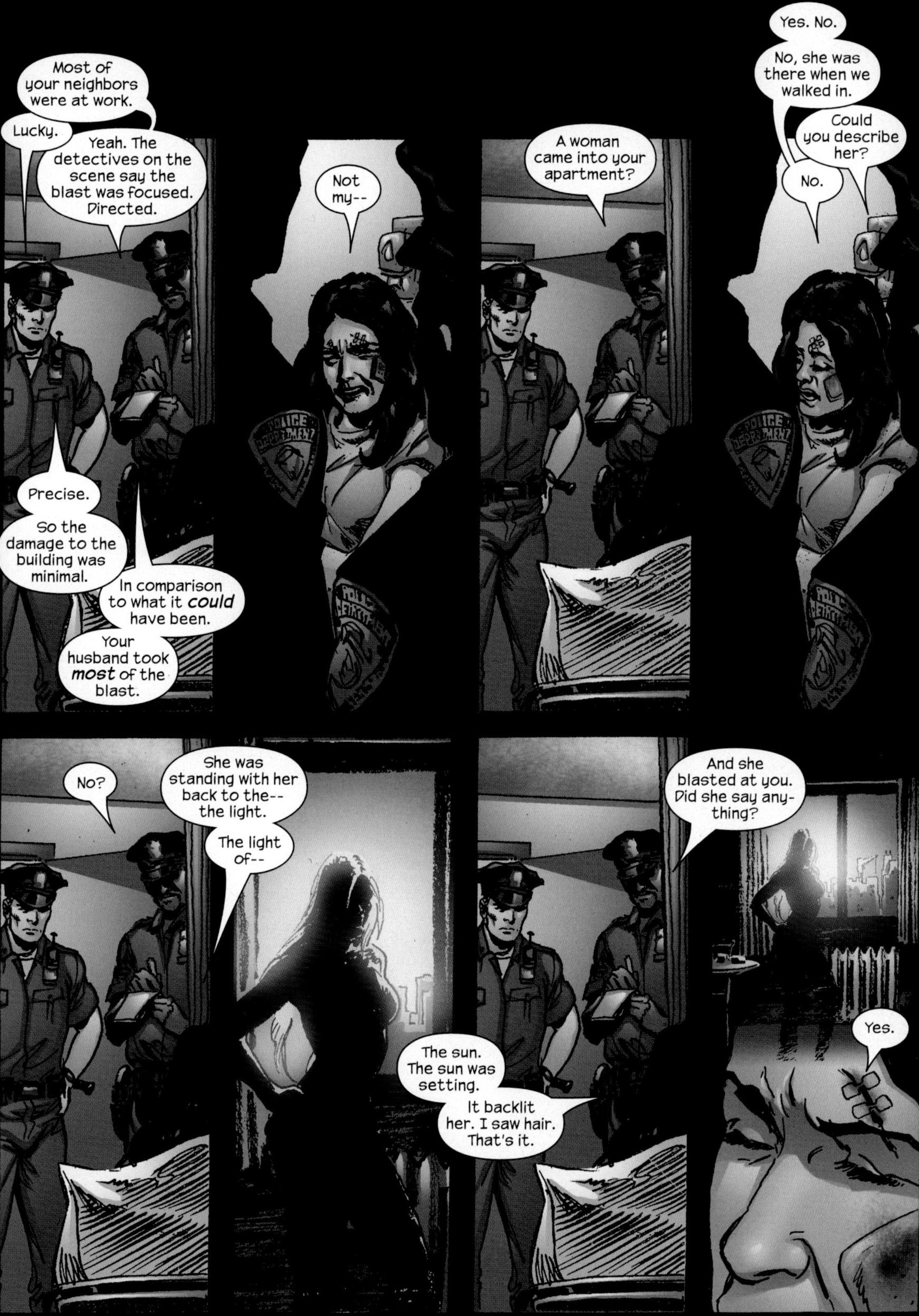

Most of your neighbors were at work.
Lucky.
Yeah. The detectives on the scene say the blast was focused. Directed.
Precise.
So the damage to the building was minimal.
In comparison to what it *could* have been.
Your husband took *most* of the blast.
Not my--
A woman came into your apartment?
Yes. No.
No, she was there when we walked in.
Could you describe her?
No.
No?
She was standing with her back to the-- the light.
The light of--
The sun. The sun was setting.
It backlit her. I saw hair. That's it.
And she blasted at you. Did she say anything?
Yes.

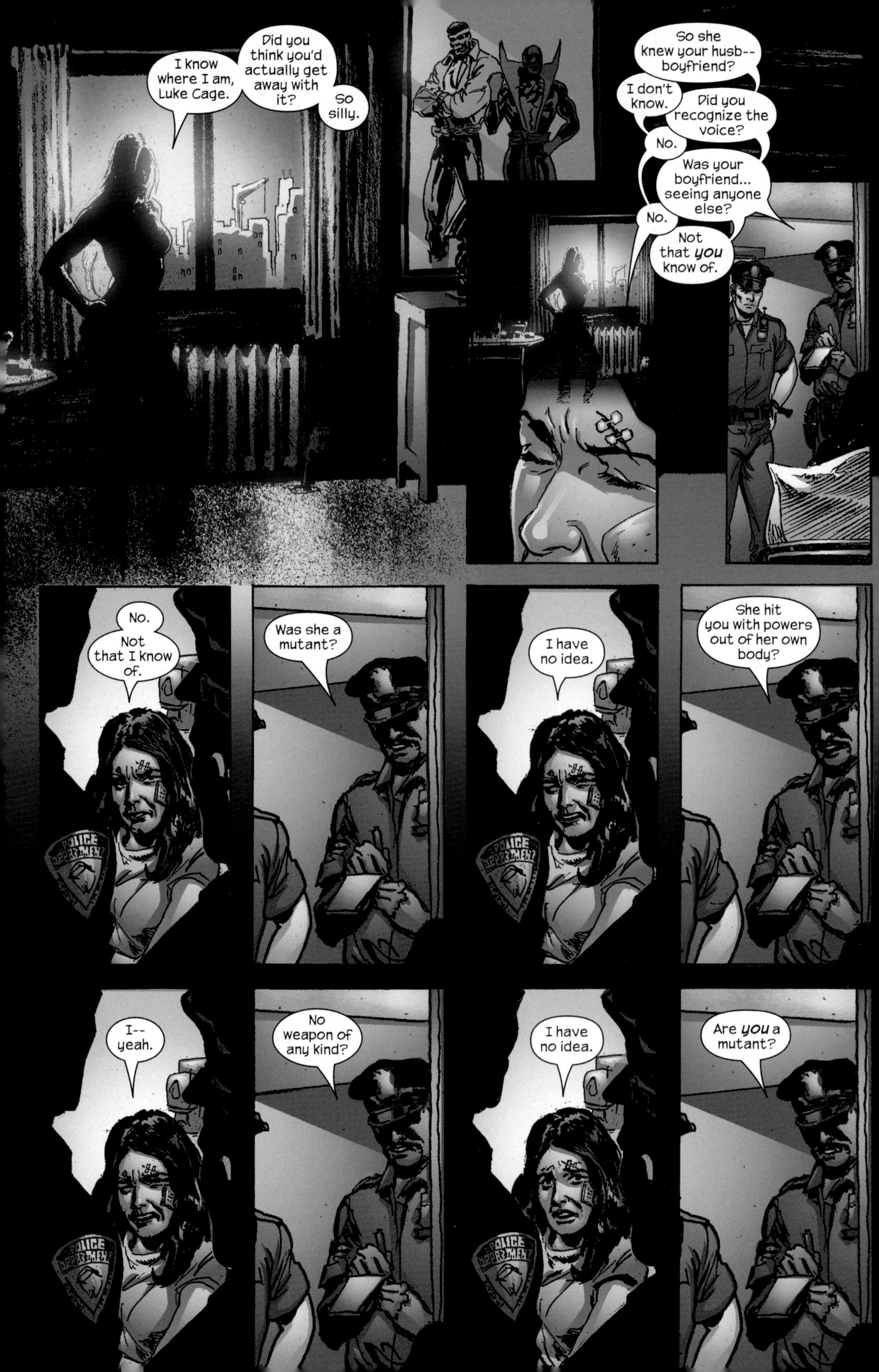

I know where I am, Luke Cage.
Did you think you'd actually get away with it?
So silly.
So she knew your husb-- boyfriend?
I don't know.
Did you recognize the voice?
No.
Was your boyfriend... seeing anyone else?
No.
Not that *you* know of.
No. Not that I know of.
Was she a mutant?
I have no idea.
She hit you with powers out of her own body?
I-- yeah.
No weapon of any kind?
I have no idea.
Are *you* a mutant?

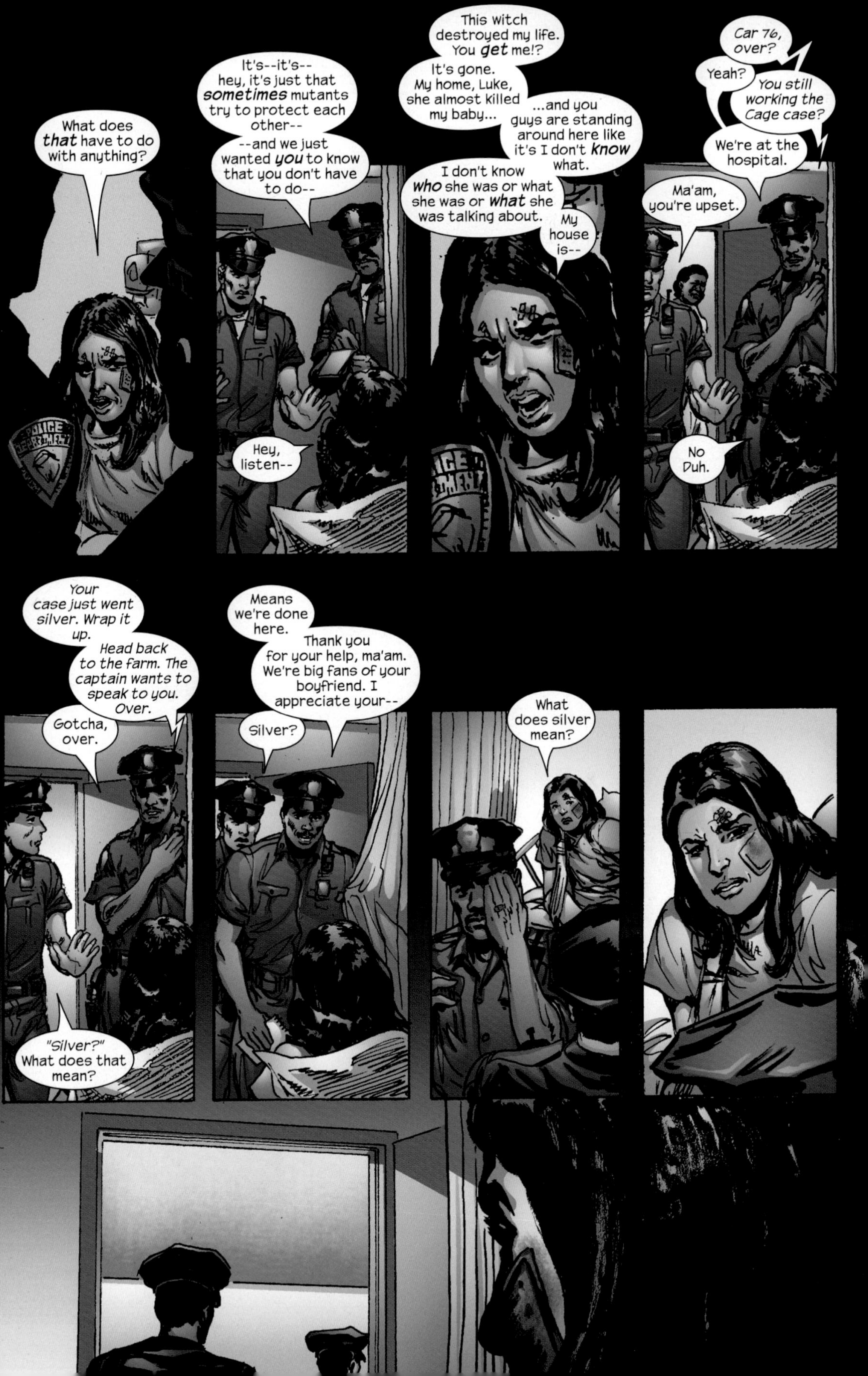
What does *that* have to do with anything?
It's--it's-- hey, it's just that *sometimes* mutants try to protect each other--
--and we just wanted *you* to know that you don't have to do--
Hey, listen--
This witch destroyed my life. You *get* me!?
It's gone. My home, Luke, she almost killed my baby...
...and you guys are standing around here like it's I don't *know* what.
I don't know *who* she was or what she was or *what* she was talking about.
My house is--
Car 76, over?
Yeah?
You still working the Cage case?
We're at the hospital.
Ma'am, you're upset.
No Duh.
Your case just went silver. Wrap it up.
Head back to the farm. The captain wants to speak to you. Over.
Gotcha, over.
"Silver?" What does that mean?
Means we're done here.
Thank you for your help, ma'am. We're big fans of your boyfriend. I appreciate your--
Silver?
What does silver mean?

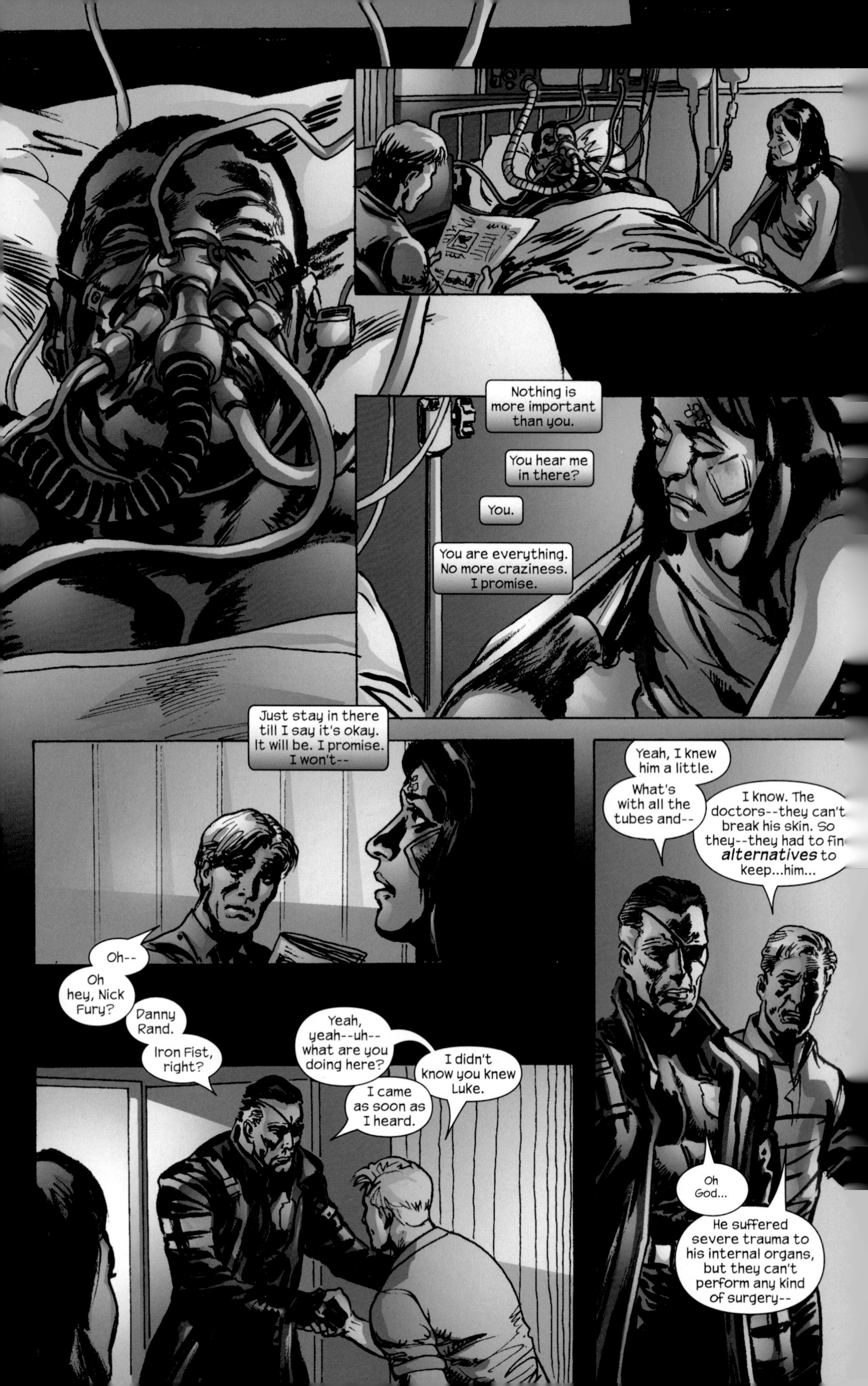
Nothing is more important than you.
You hear me in there?
You.
You are everything. No more craziness. I promise.
Just stay in there till I say it's okay. It will be. I promise. I won't--
Oh--
Oh hey, Nick Fury?
Danny Rand.
Iron Fist, right?
Yeah, yeah--uh-- what are you doing here?
I came as soon as I heard.
I didn't know you knew Luke.
Yeah, I knew him a little.
What's with all the tubes and--
I know. The doctors--they can't break his skin. So they--they had to fin alternatives to keep...him...
Oh God...
He suffered severe trauma to his internal organs, but they can't perform any kind of surgery--

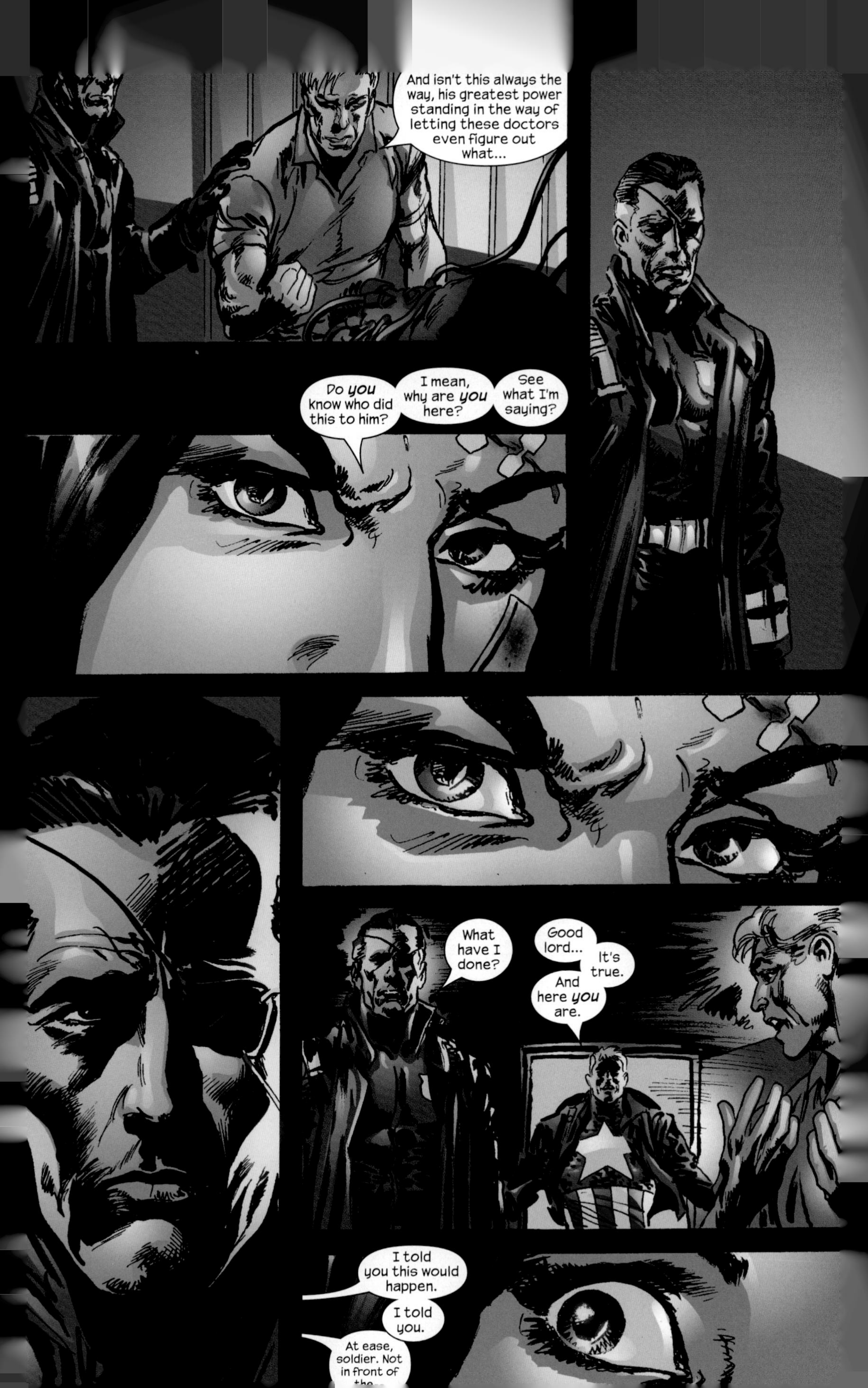
And isn't this always the way, his greatest power standing in the way of letting these doctors even figure out what...
Do *you* know who did this to him?
I mean, why are *you* here?
See what I'm saying?
What have I done?
Good lord...
It's true.
And here *you* are.
I told you this would happen.
I told you.
At ease, soldier. Not in front of

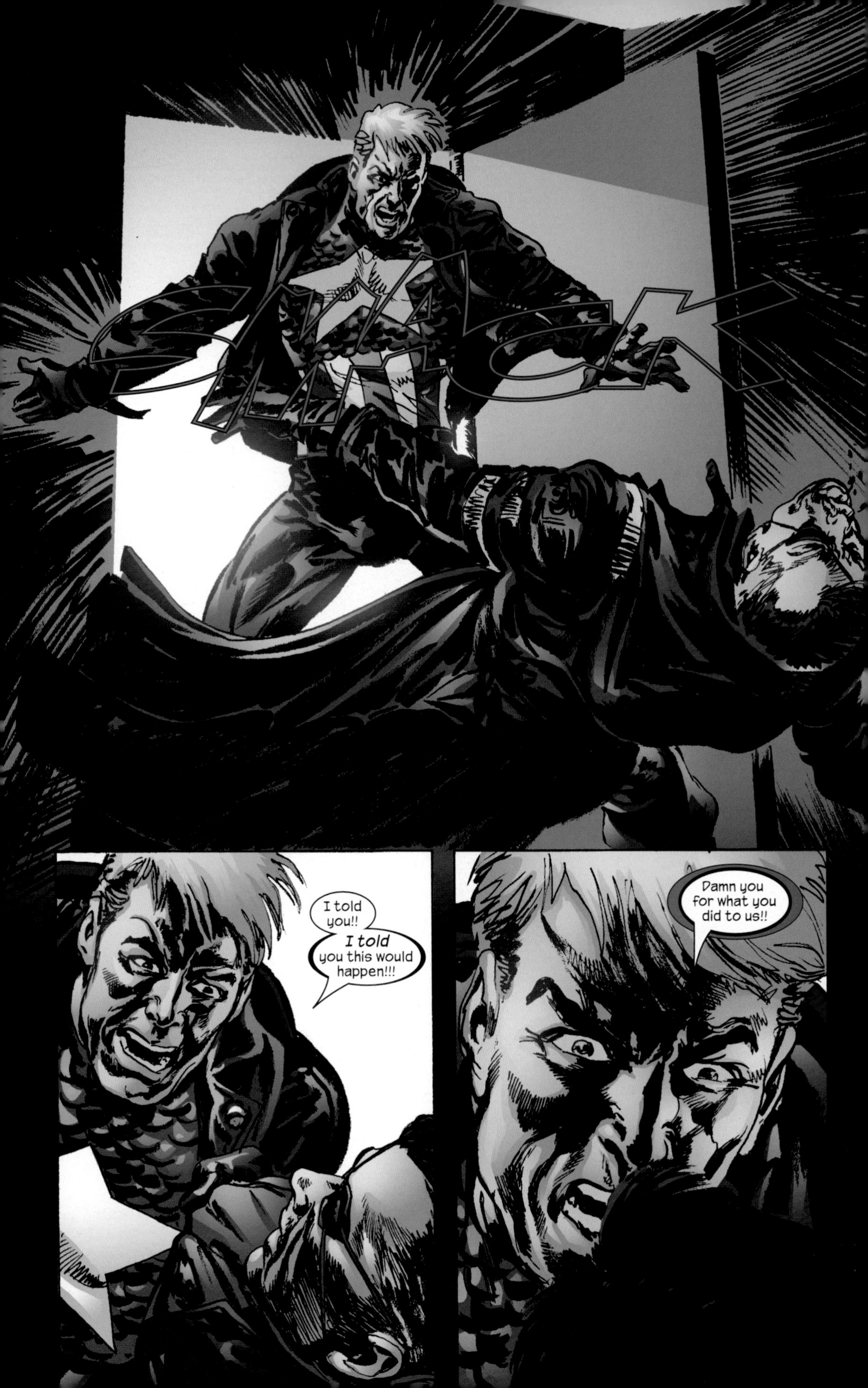
I told you!!
I told you this would happen!!!
Damn you for what you did to us!!

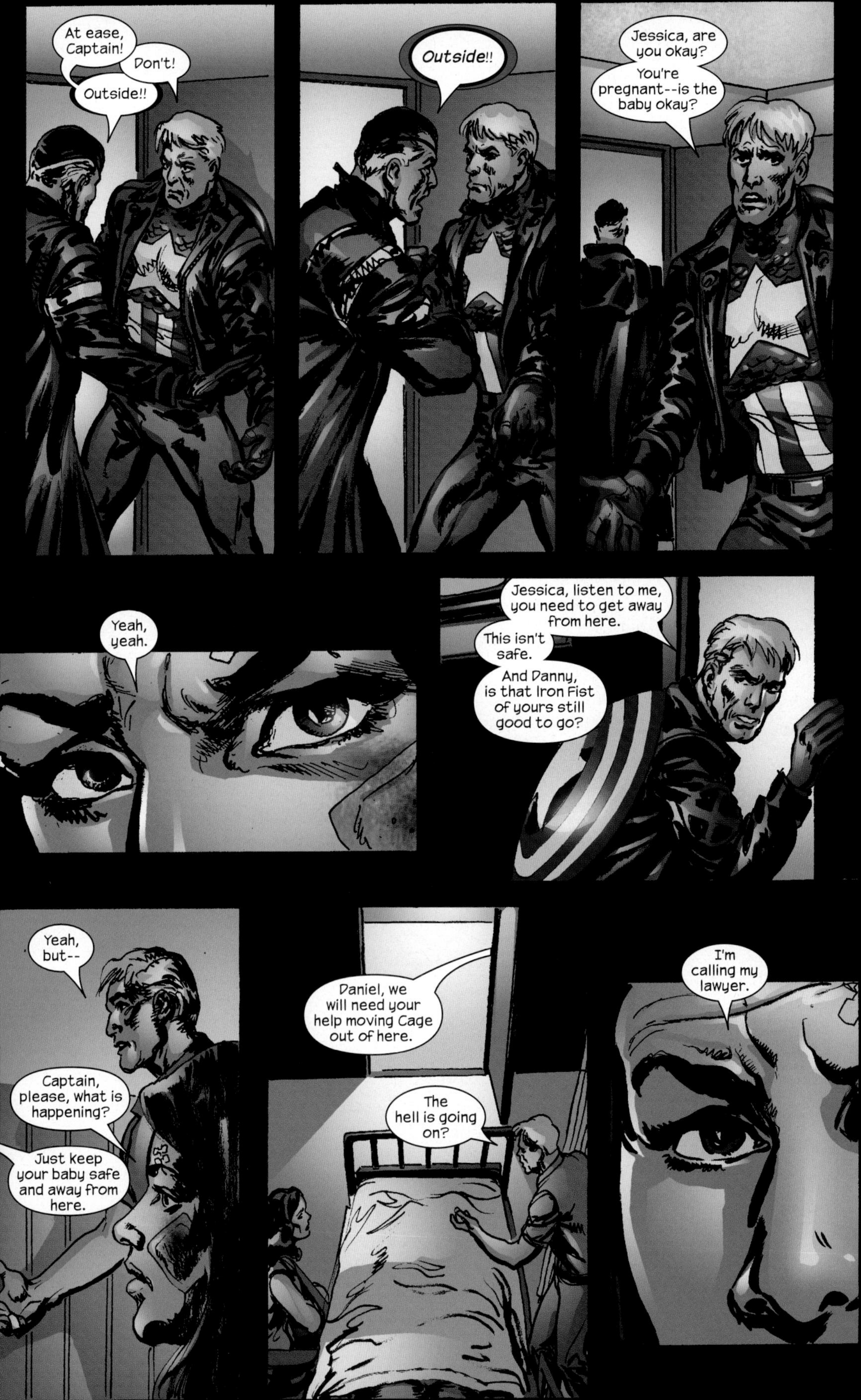
At ease, Captain!
Don't!
Outside!!
Outside!!
Jessica, are you okay?
You're pregnant--is the baby okay?
Yeah, yeah.
Jessica, listen to me, you need to get away from here.
This isn't safe.
And Danny, is that Iron Fist of yours still good to go?
Yeah, but--
Captain, please, what is happening?
Just keep your baby safe and away from here.
Daniel, we will need your help moving Cage out of here.
The hell is going on?
I'm calling my lawyer.

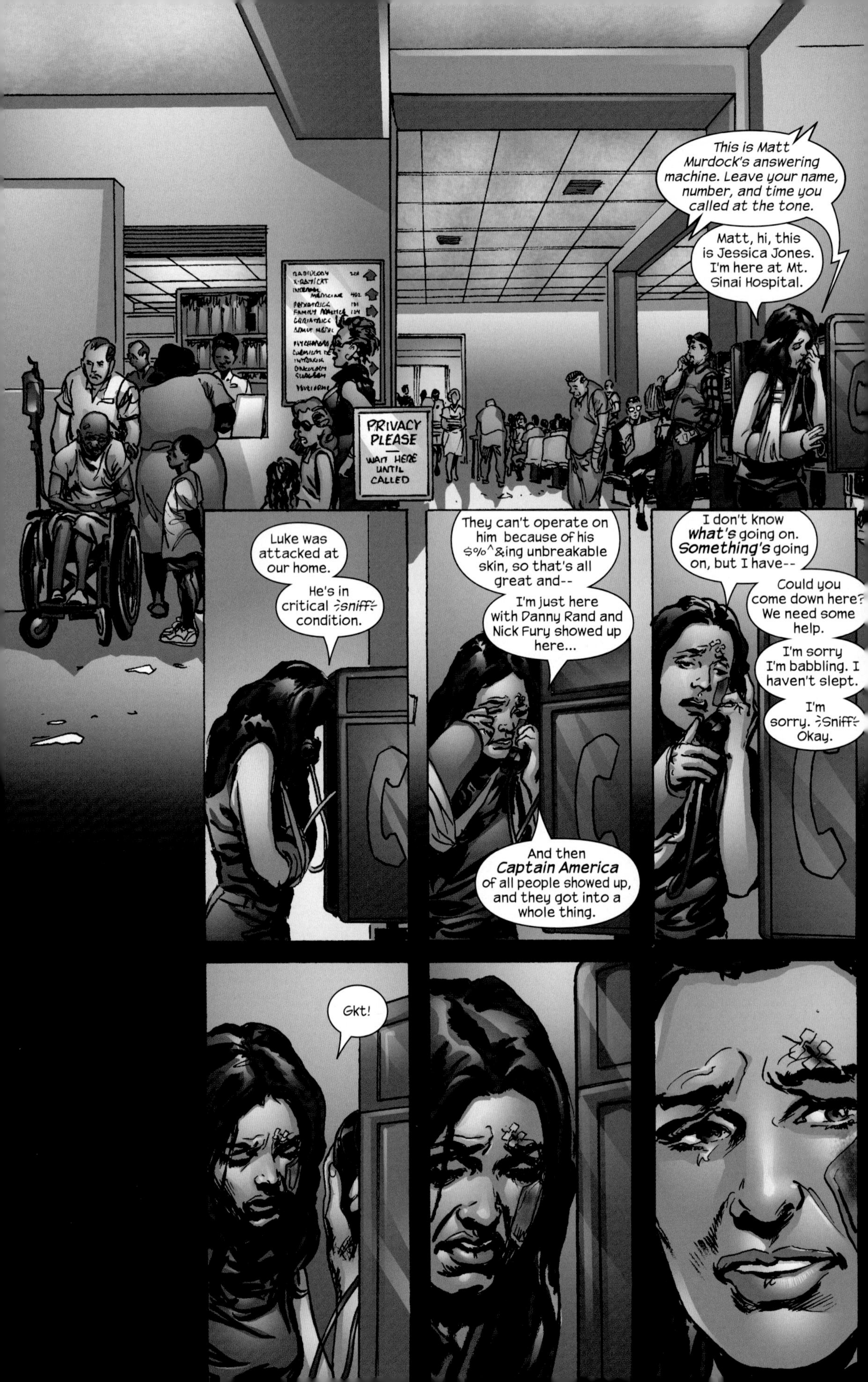

This is Matt Murdock's answering machine. Leave your name, number, and time you called at the tone.
Matt, hi, this is Jessica Jones. I'm here at Mt. Sinai Hospital.
PRIVACY PLEASE
WAIT HERE UNTIL CALLED
Luke was attacked at our home.
He's in critical ~sniff~ condition.
They can't operate on him because of his $%^&ing unbreakable skin, so that's all great and--
I'm just here with Danny Rand and Nick Fury showed up here...
And then *Captain America* of all people showed up, and they got into a whole thing.
I don't know *what's* going on. *Something's* going on, but I have--
Could you come down here? We need some help.
I'm sorry I'm babbling. I haven't slept.
I'm sorry. ~Sniff~ Okay.
Gkt!

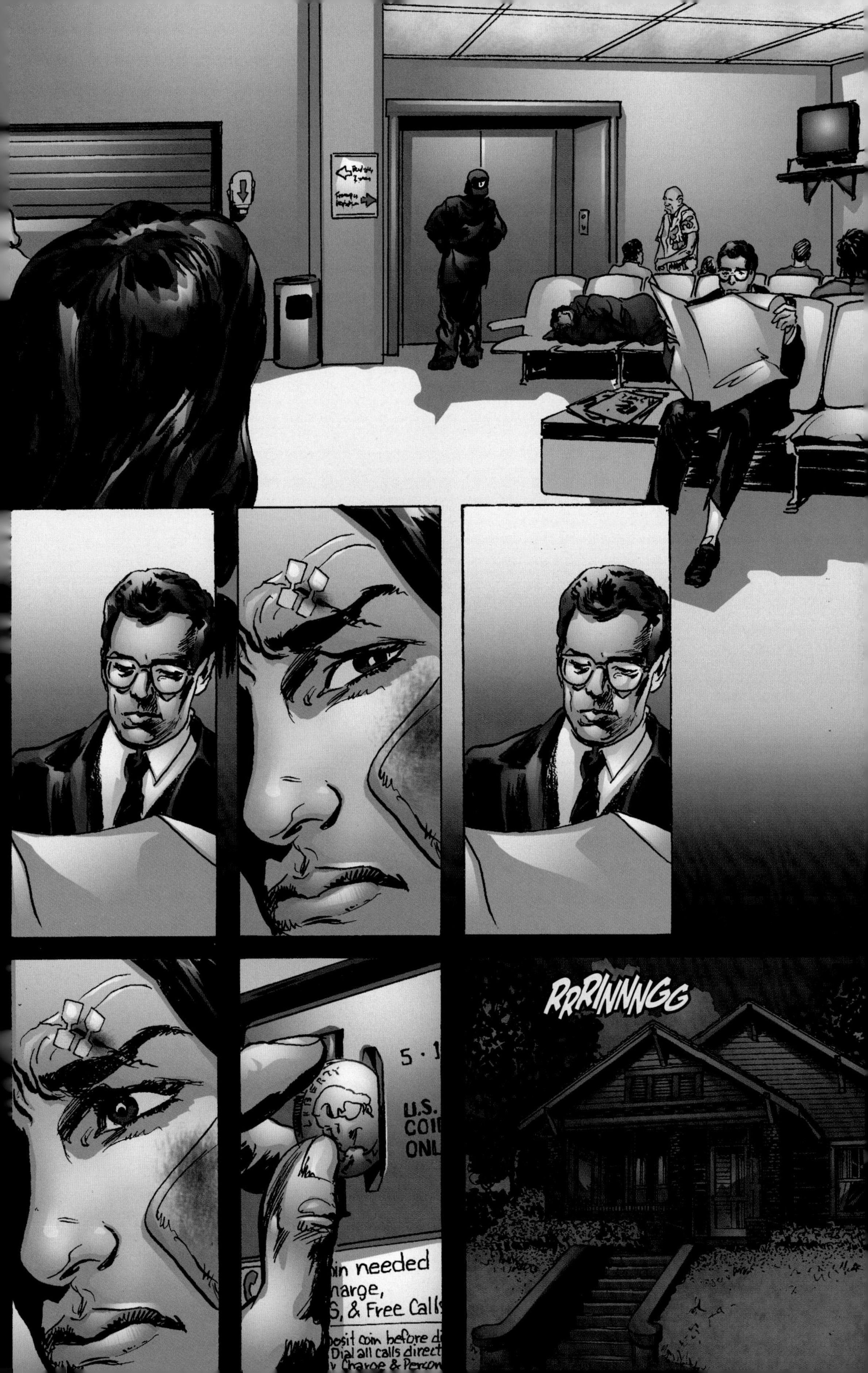
5 · 1
U.S.
COI
ONL
in needed
arge,
S, & Free Calls
posit coin before d
Dial all calls direct
RRRINNNGG

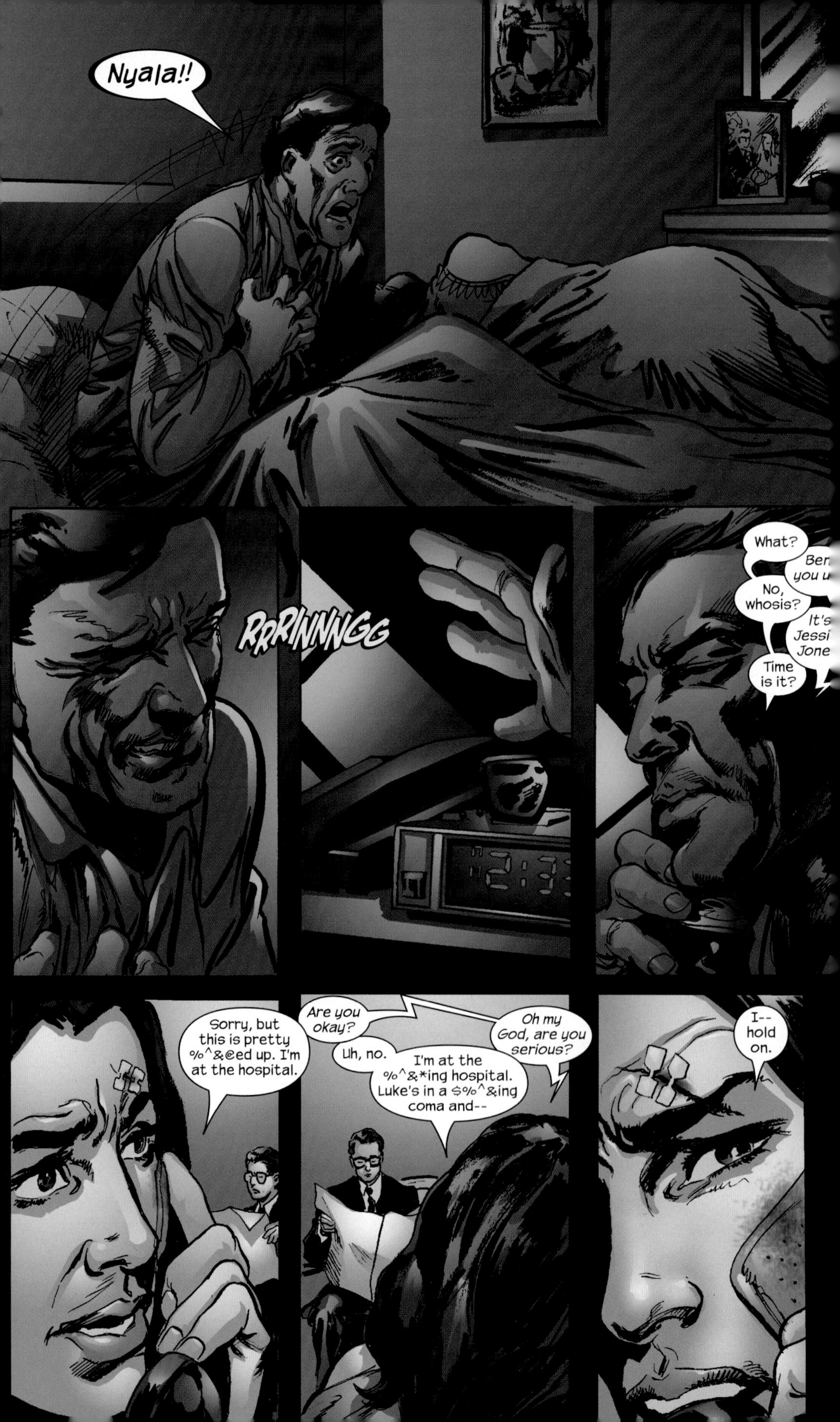

Nyala!!
RRRINNNGG
What?
No, whosis?
It's
Time is it?
Sorry, but this is pretty %^&@ed up. I'm at the hospital.
Are you okay?
Uh, no.
Oh my God, are you serious?
I'm at the %^&*ing hospital. Luke's in a $%^&ing coma and--
I-- hold on.

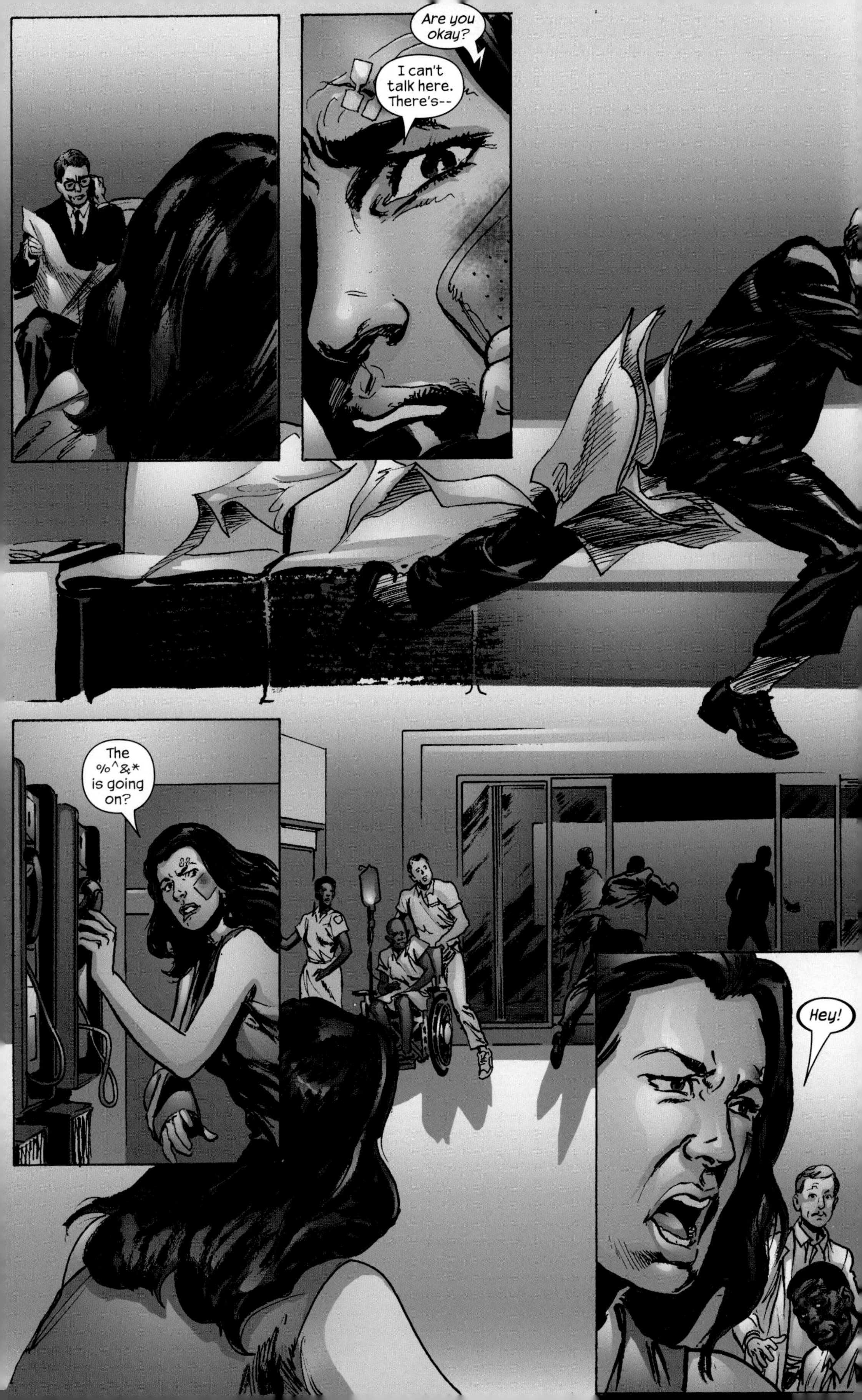

Are you okay?
I can't talk here. There's--
The %^&* is going on?
Hey!

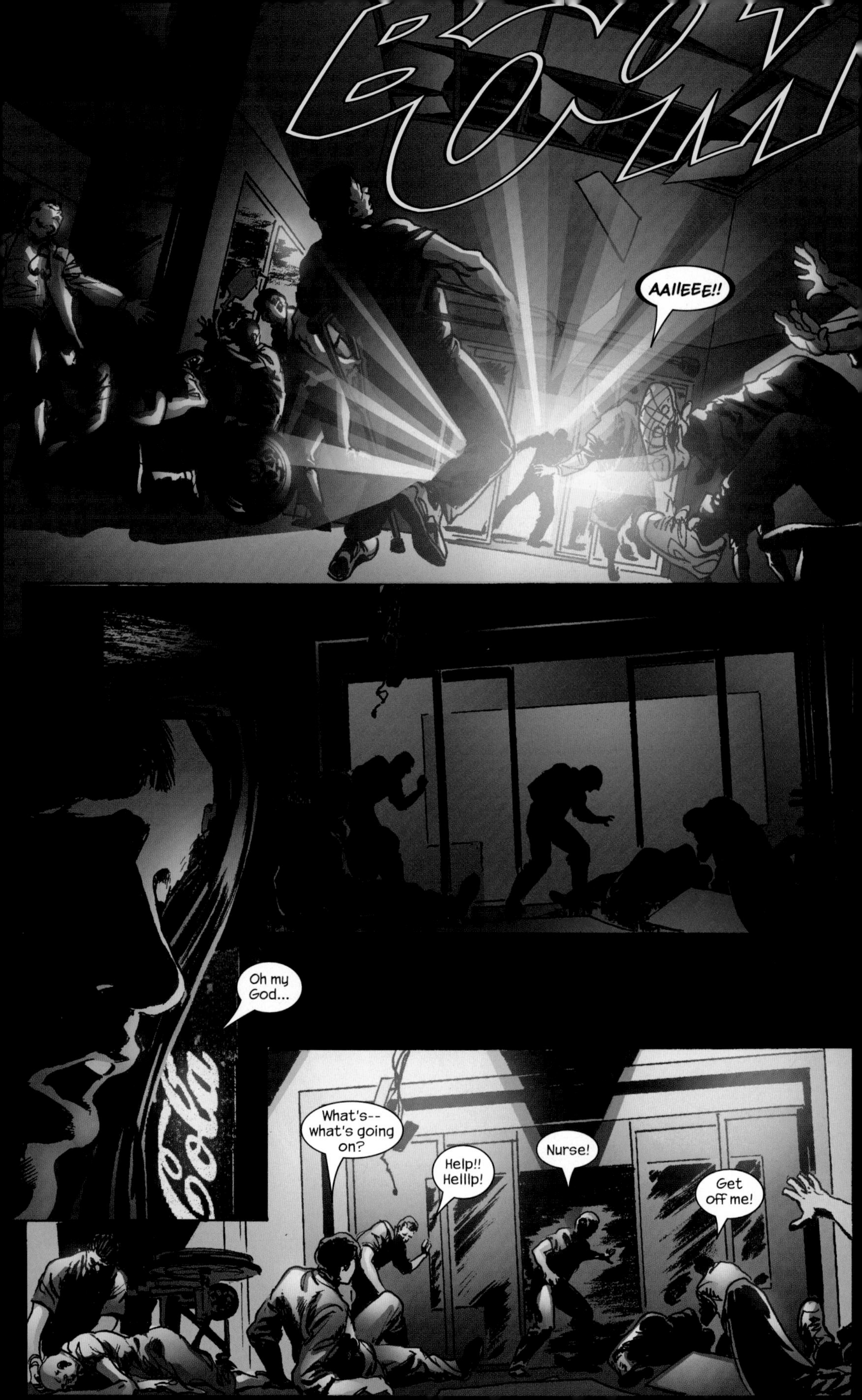
AAIIEEE!!
Oh my God...
What's-- what's going on?
Help!! Helllp!
Nurse!
Get off me!

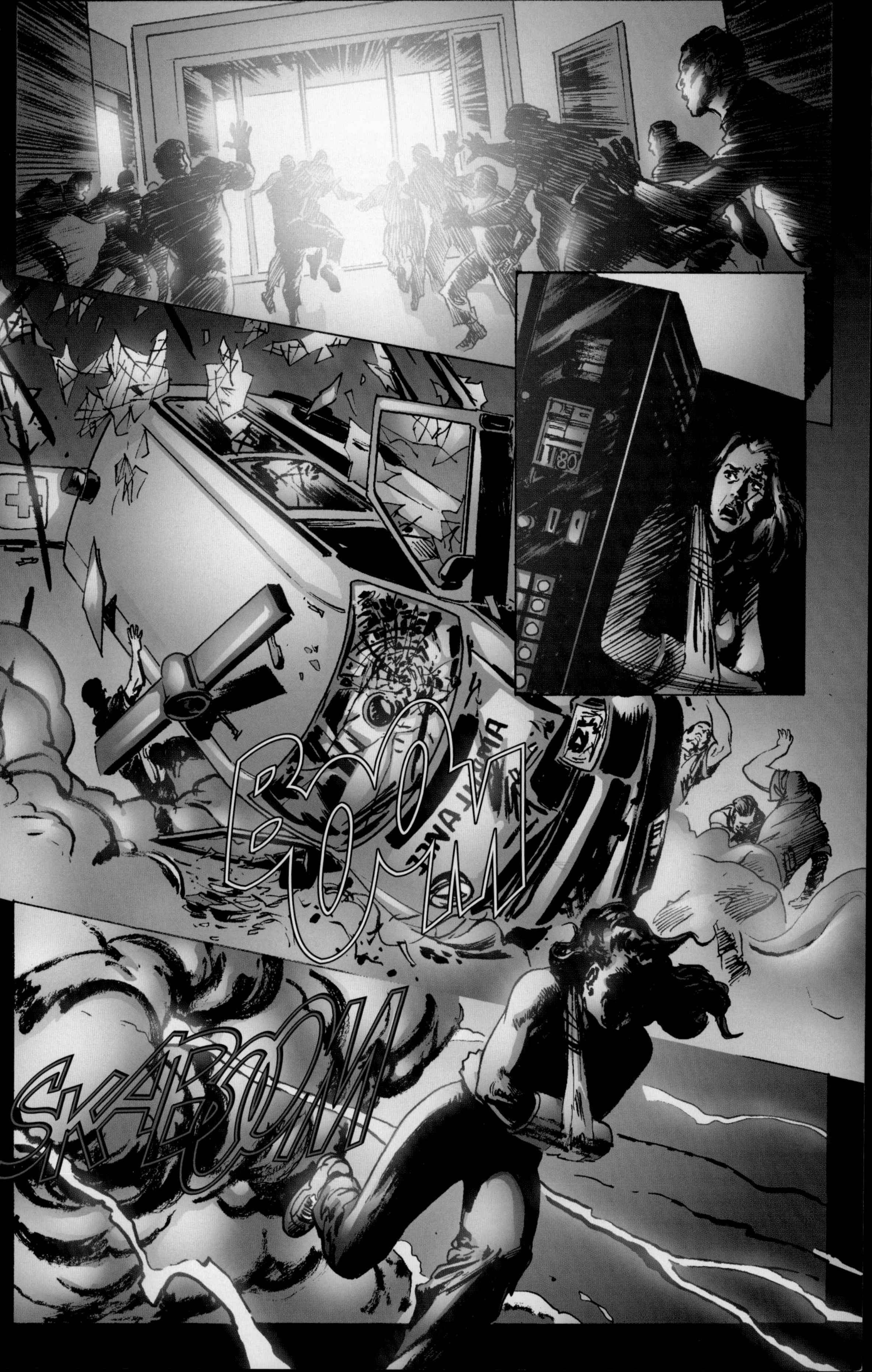
BOOM
SKABOOM

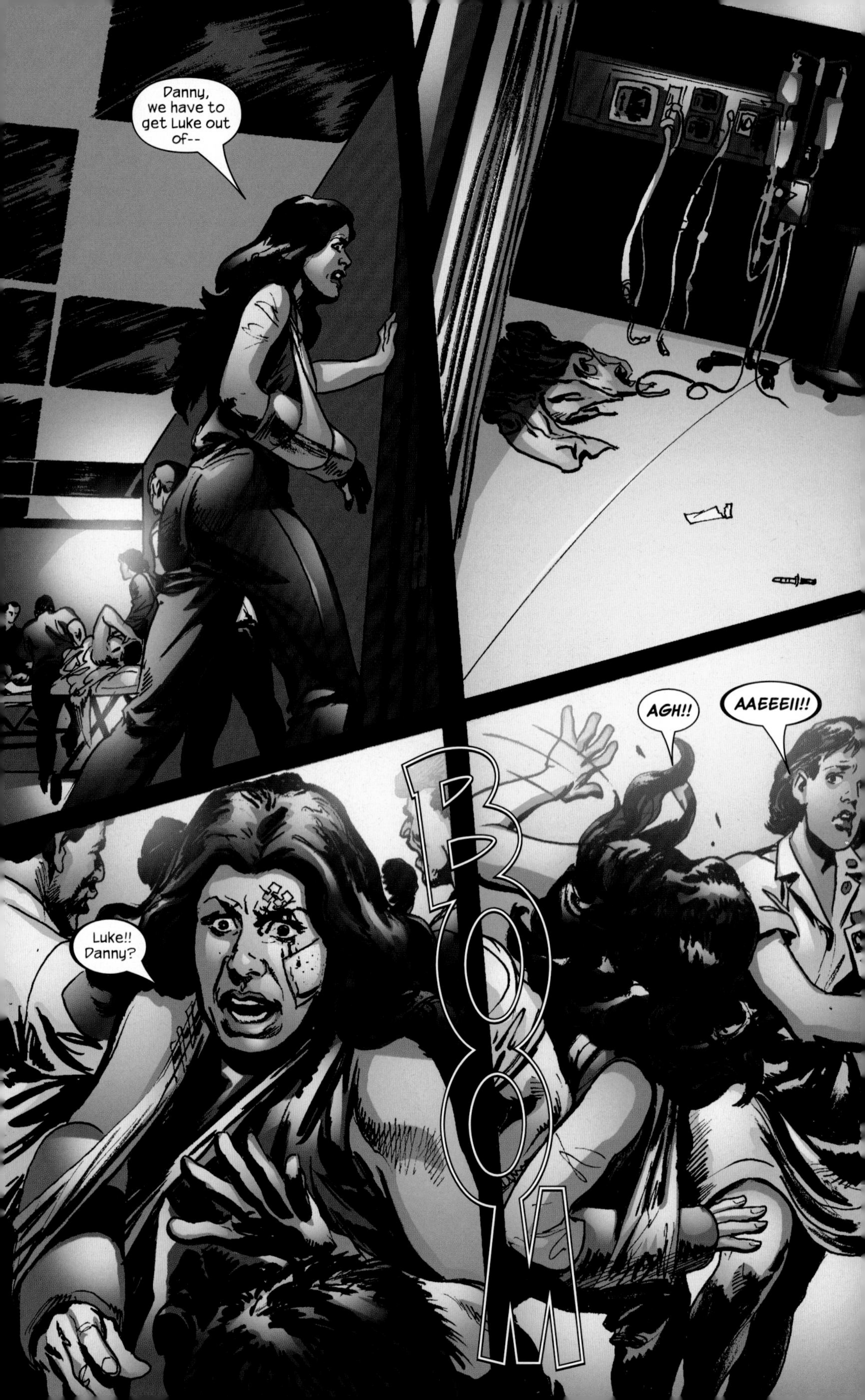
Danny, we have to get Luke out of--
AGH!!
AAEEEII!!
BOOM
Luke!! Danny?

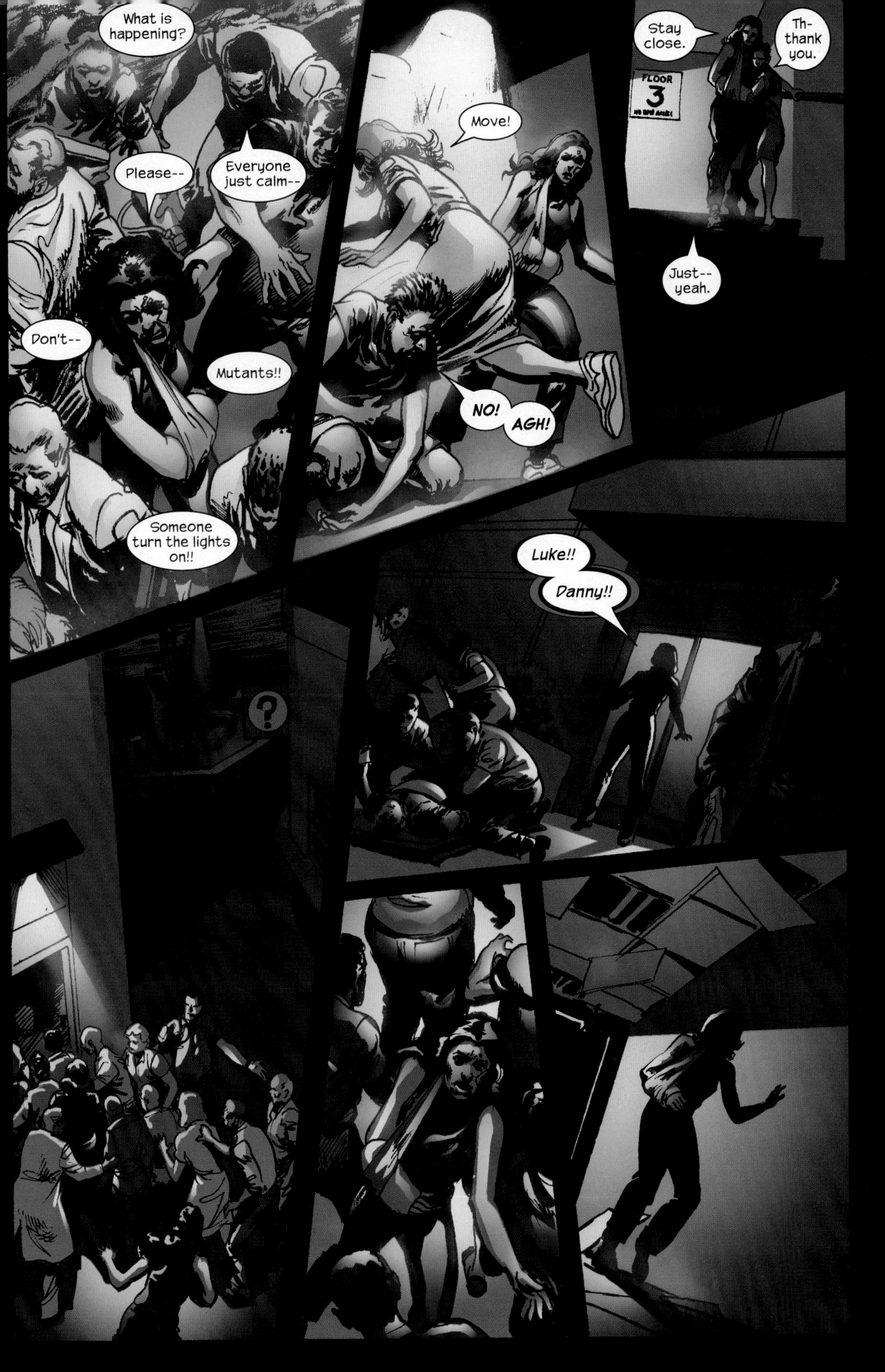
What is happening?
Please--
Everyone just calm--
Don't--
Mutants!!
Someone turn the lights on!!
Move!
NO!
AGH!
Stay close.
Th-thank you.
FLOOR 3
Just--yeah.
Luke!!
Danny!!

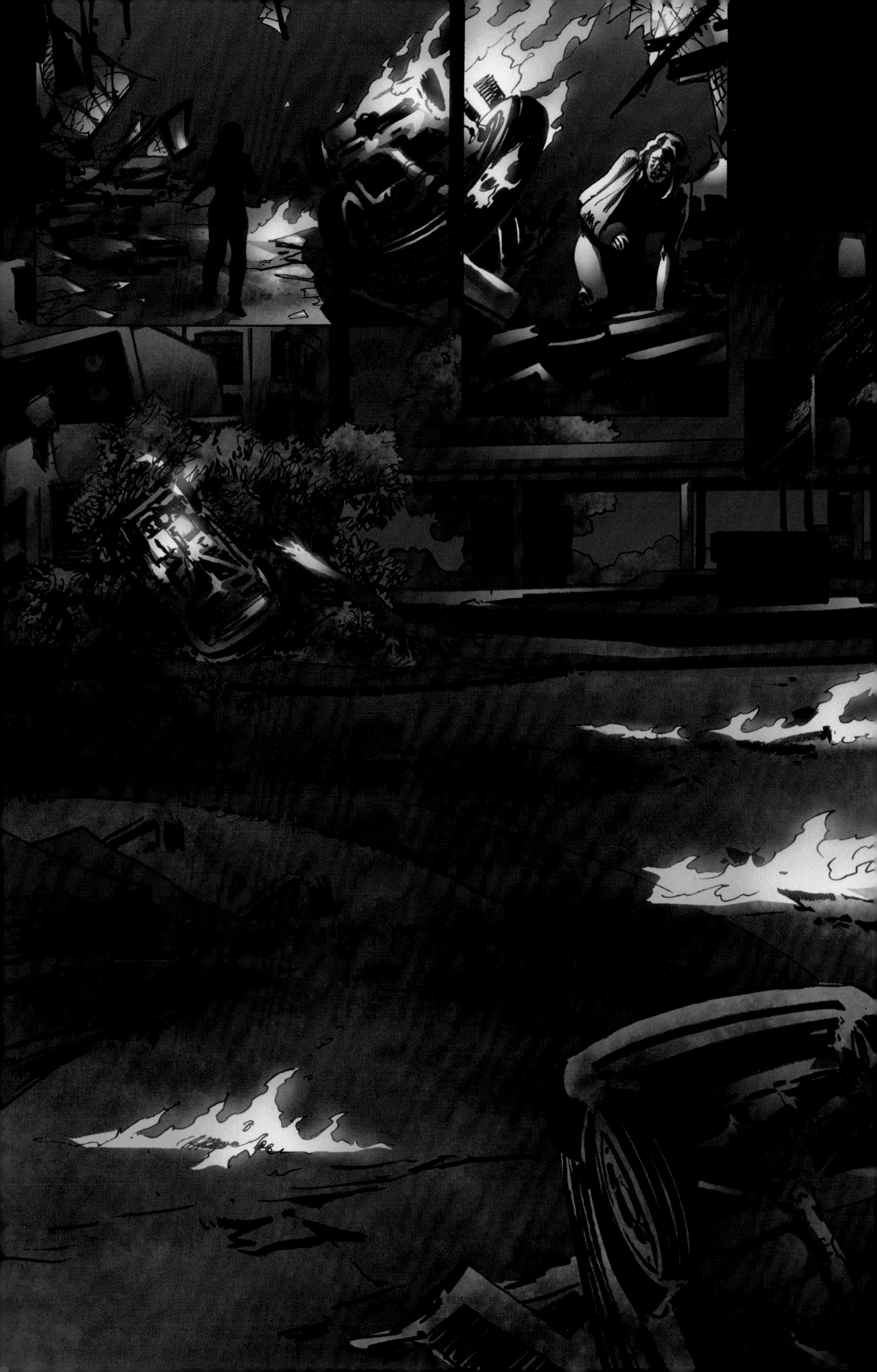

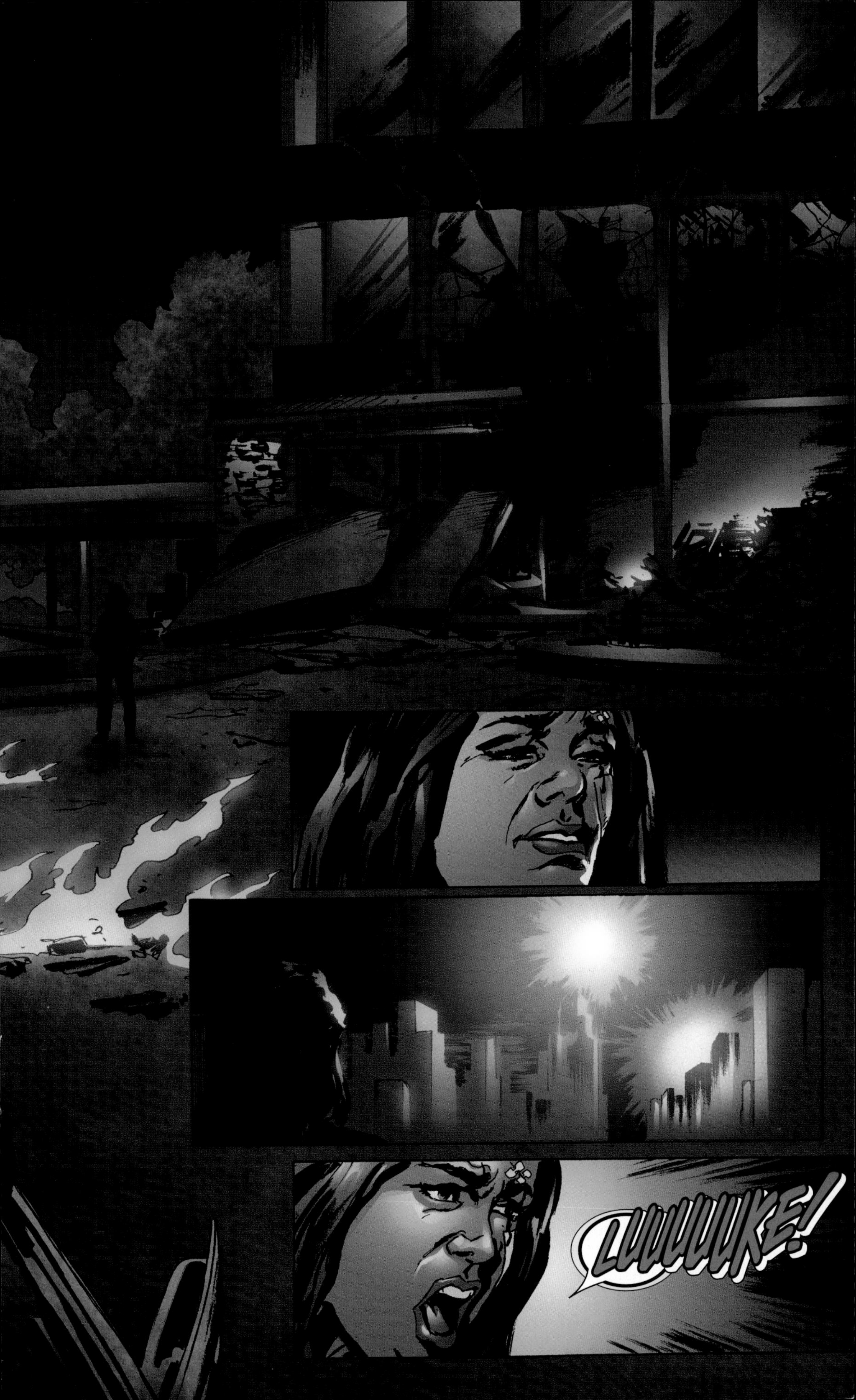
LUUUUUKE!

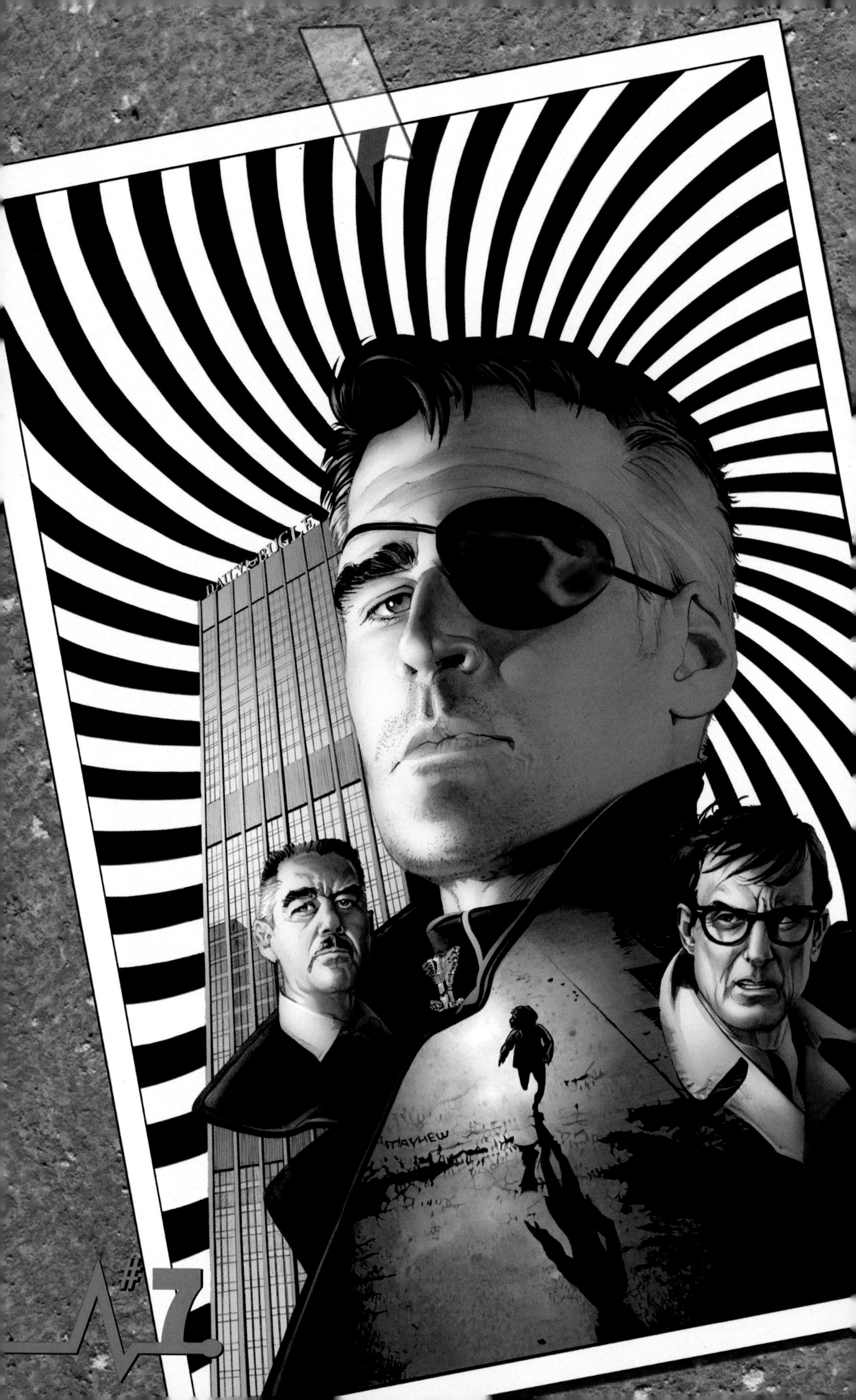
DAILY BUGLE
MAYHEW
#7

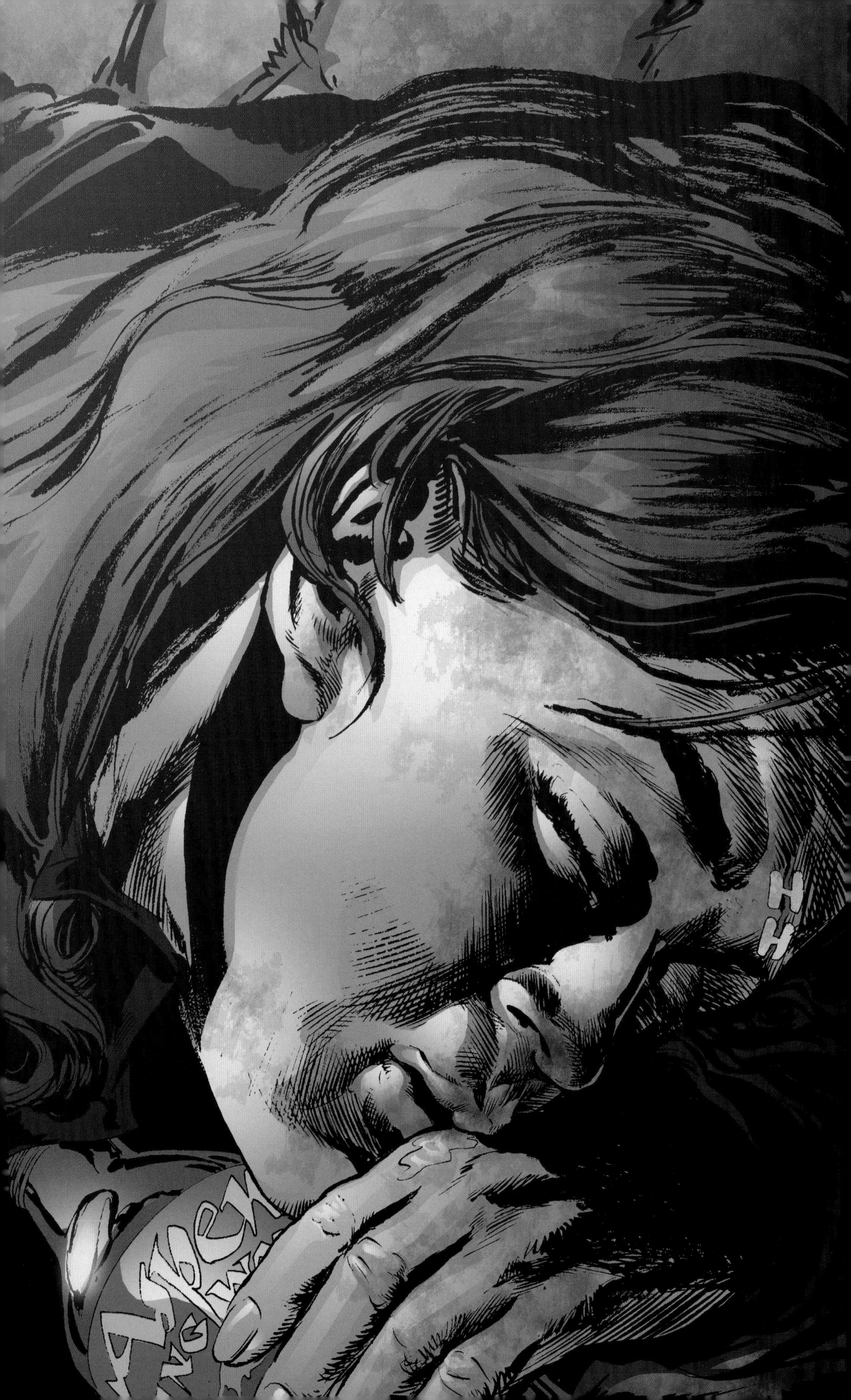

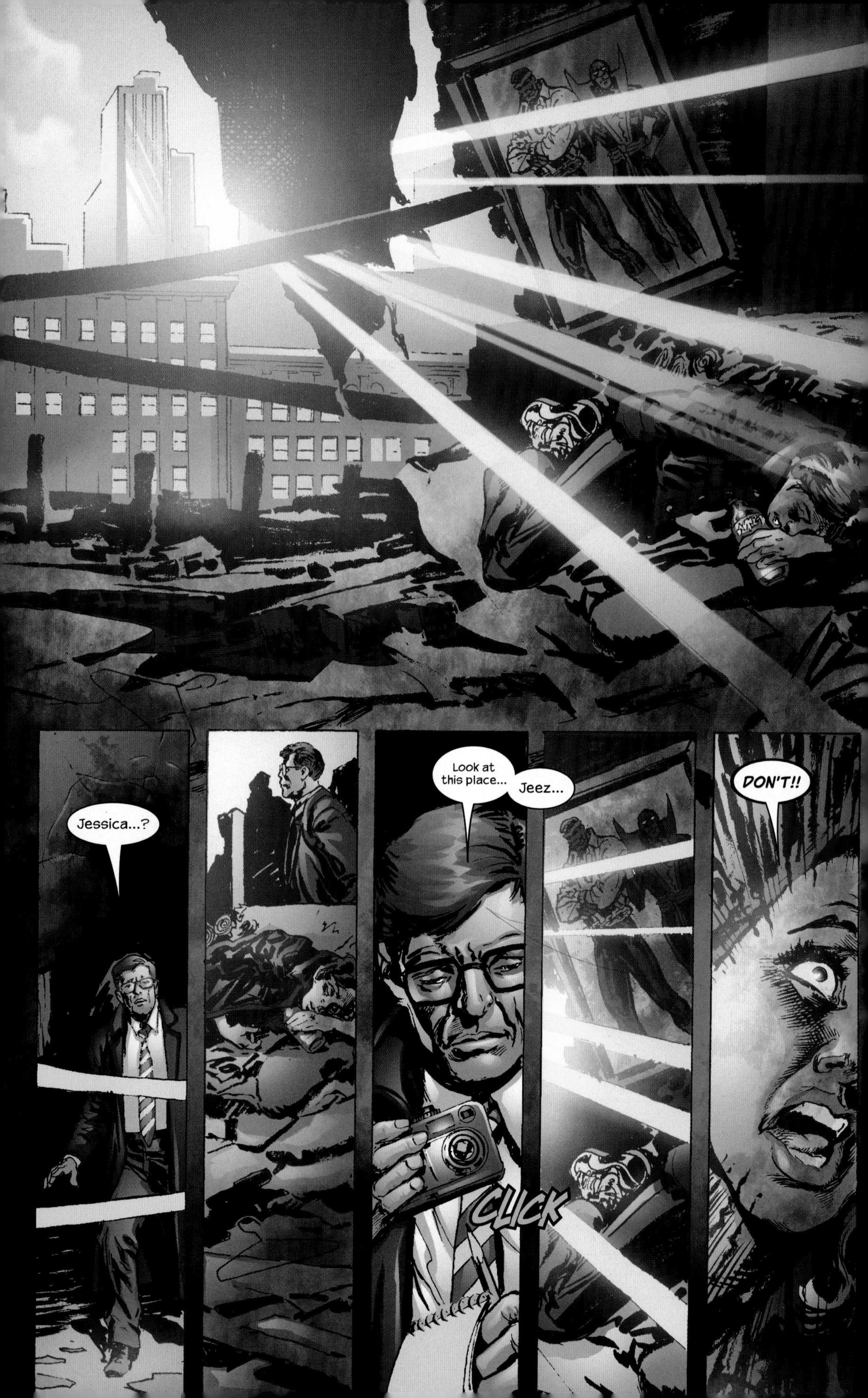
Jessica...?
Look at this place...
Jeez...
CLICK
DON'T!!

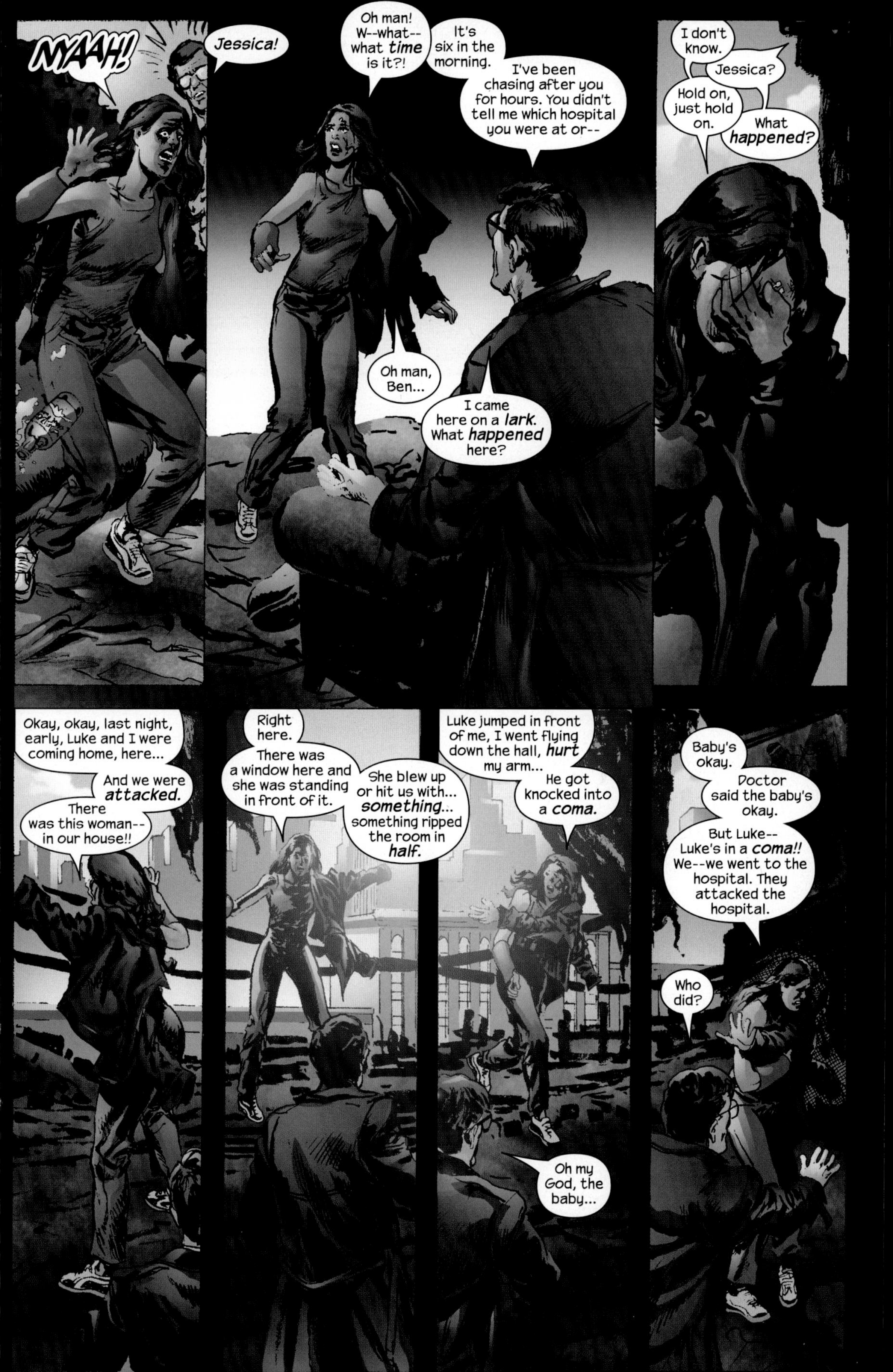
NYAAH!
Jessica!
Oh man! W--what-- what time is it?!
It's six in the morning.
I've been chasing after you for hours. You didn't tell me which hospital you were at or--
Oh man, Ben...
I came here on a lark. What happened here?
I don't know.
Jessica?
Hold on, just hold on.
What happened?
Okay, okay, last night, early, Luke and I were coming home, here...
And we were attacked.
There was this woman-- in our house!!
Right here.
There was a window here and she was standing in front of it.
She blew up or hit us with... something... something ripped the room in half.
Luke jumped in front of me, I went flying down the hall, hurt my arm...
He got knocked into a coma.
Oh my God, the baby...
Baby's okay.
Doctor said the baby's okay.
But Luke-- Luke's in a coma!! We--we went to the hospital. They attacked the hospital.
Who did?

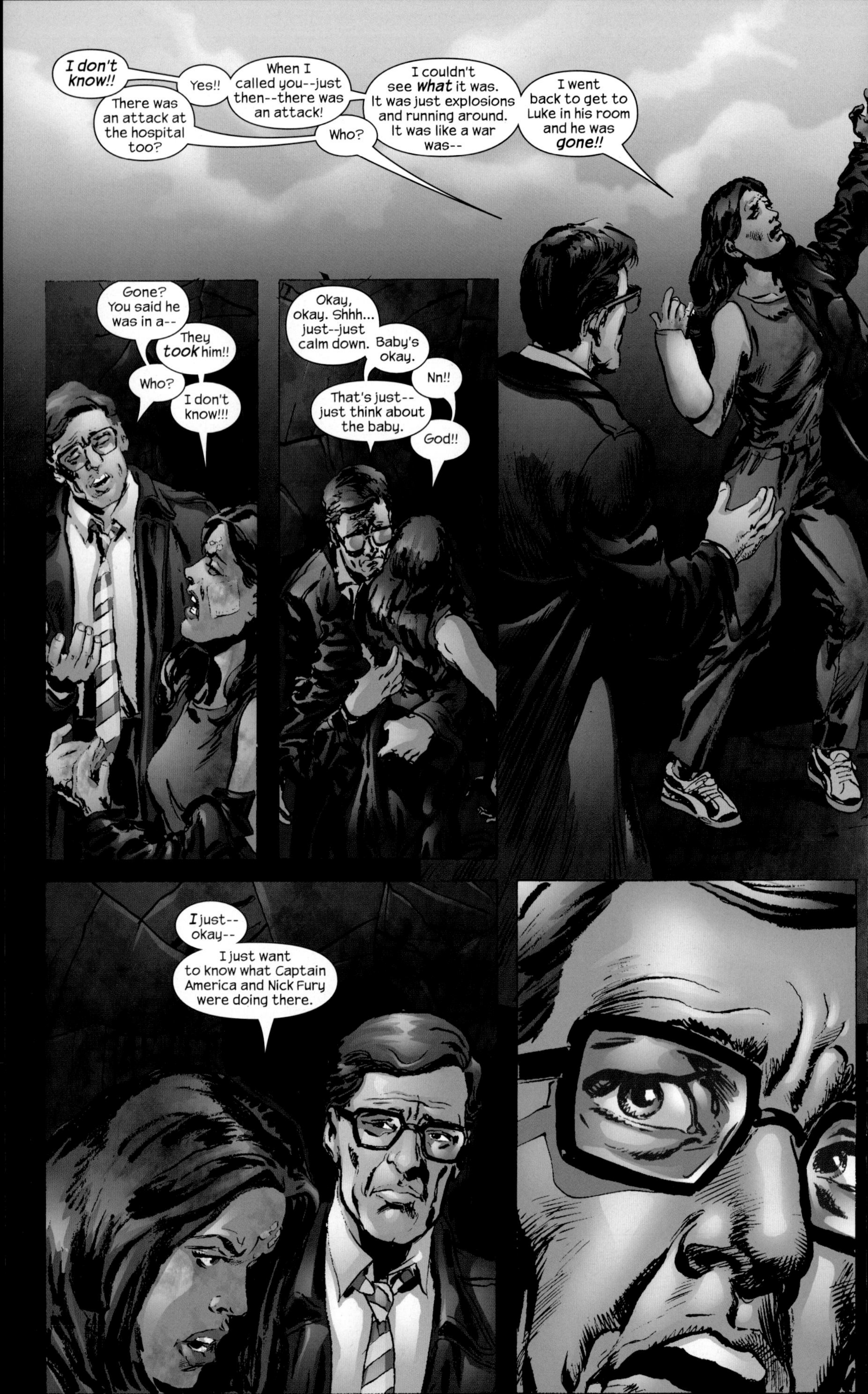
I don't know!!
Yes!!
There was an attack at the hospital too?
When I called you--just then--there was an attack!
Who?
I couldn't see what it was. It was just explosions and running around. It was like a war was--
I went back to get to Luke in his room and he was gone!!
Gone? You said he was in a--
They took him!!
Who?
I don't know!!!
Okay, okay. Shhh... just--just calm down.
Baby's okay.
Nn!!
That's just--just think about the baby.
God!!
I just--okay--
I just want to know what Captain America and Nick Fury were doing there.

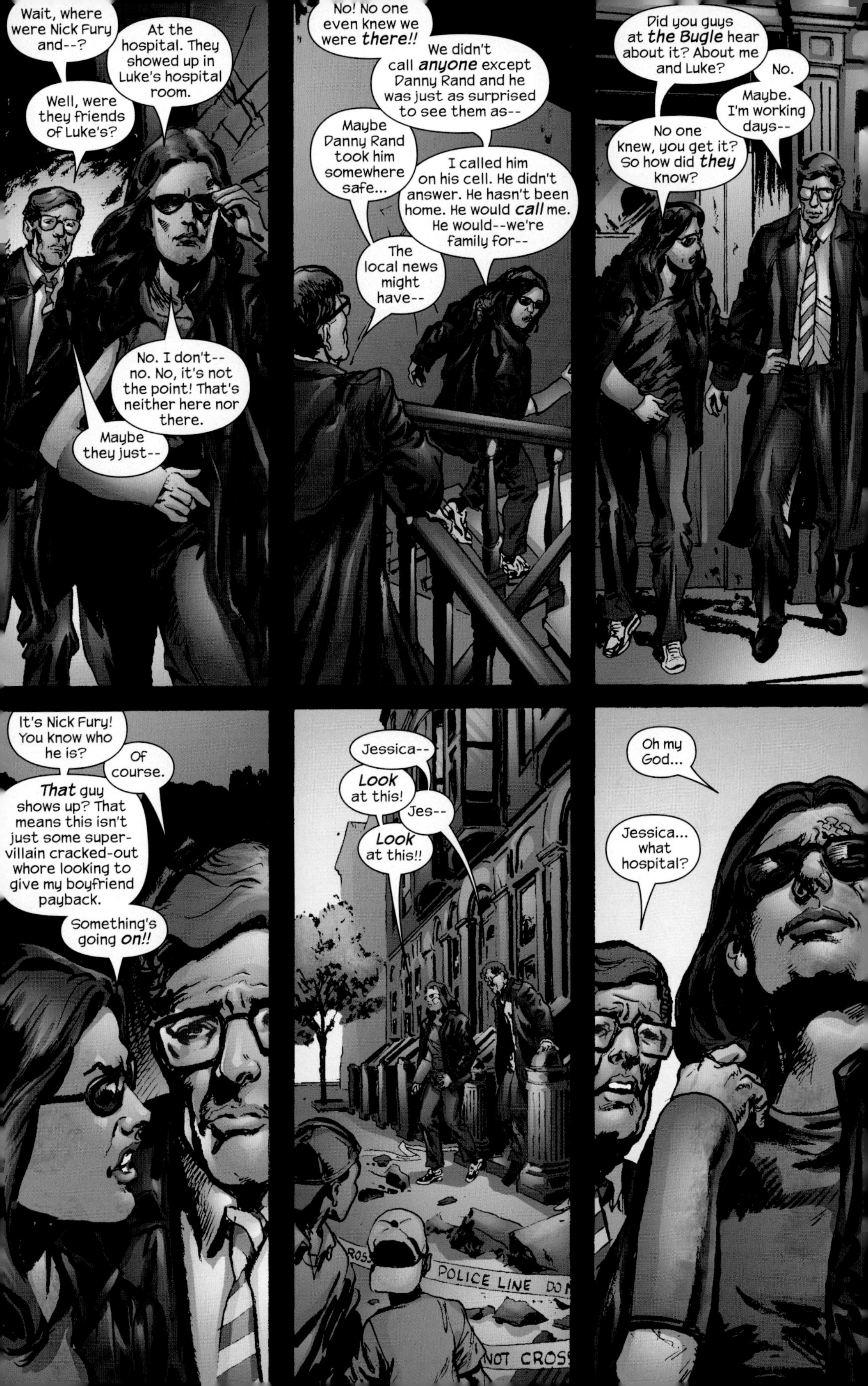

Wait, where were Nick Fury and--?
At the hospital. They showed up in Luke's hospital room.
Well, were they friends of Luke's?
No. I don't-- no. No, it's not the point! That's neither here nor there.
Maybe they just--
No! No one even knew we were *there!!*
We didn't call *anyone* except Danny Rand and he was just as surprised to see them as--
Maybe Danny Rand took him somewhere safe...
I called him on his cell. He didn't answer. He hasn't been home. He would *call* me. He would--we're family for--
The local news might have--
Did you guys at *the Bugle* hear about it? About me and Luke?
No.
Maybe. I'm working days--
No one knew, you get it? So how did *they* know?
It's Nick Fury! You know who he is?
Of course.
That guy shows up? That means this isn't just some super-villain cracked-out whore looking to give my boyfriend payback.
Something's going *on!!*
Jessica--
Look at this!
Jes--
Look at this!!
POLICE LINE DO
NOT CROSS
Oh my God...
Jessica... what hospital?

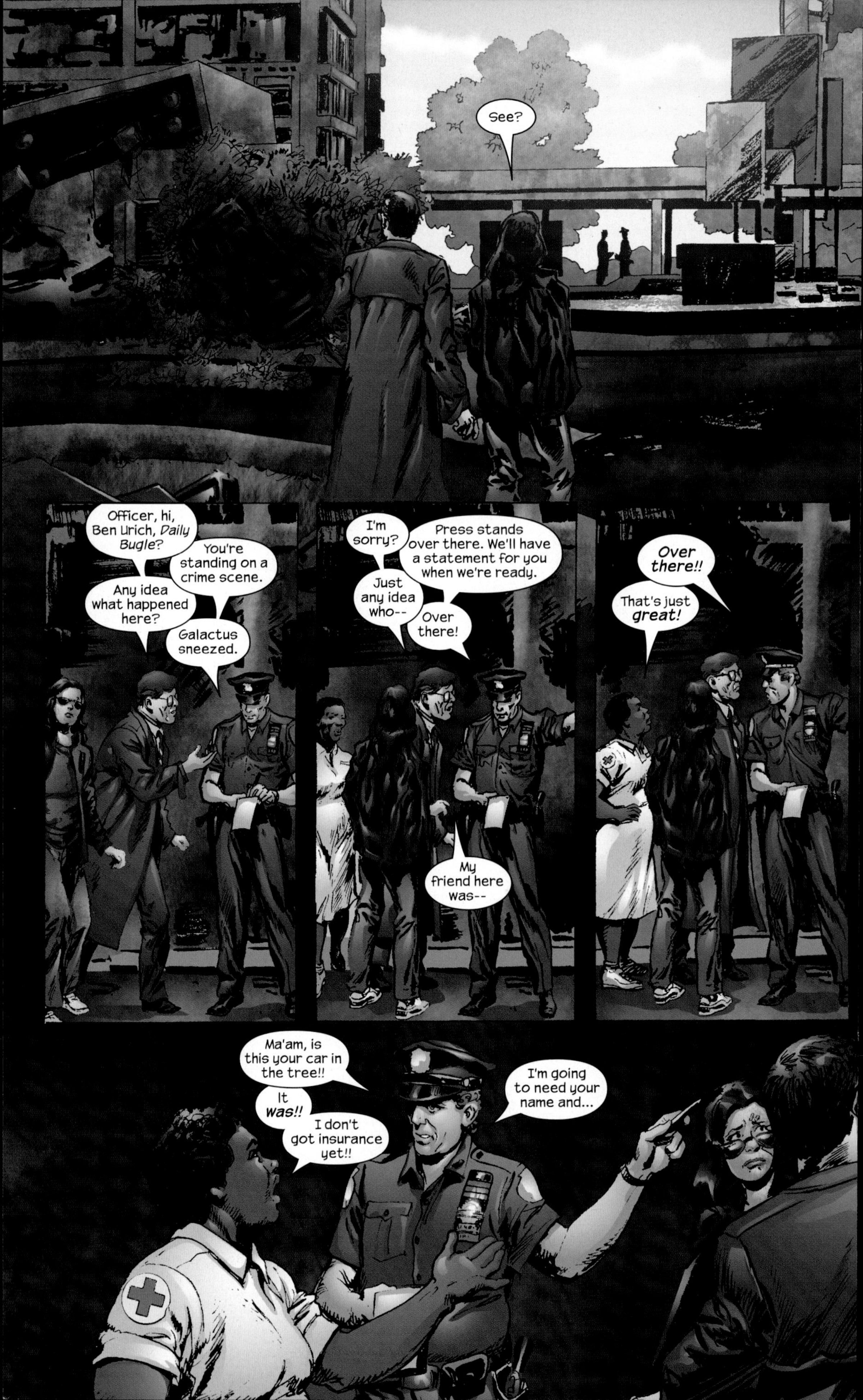
See?
Officer, hi, Ben Urich, *Daily Bugle*?
You're standing on a crime scene.
Any idea what happened here?
Galactus sneezed.
I'm sorry?
Press stands over there. We'll have a statement for you when we're ready.
Just any idea who--
Over there!
My friend here was--
Over there!!
That's just ***great!***
Ma'am, is this your car in the tree!!
It ***was!!***
I don't got insurance yet!!
I'm going to need your name and...

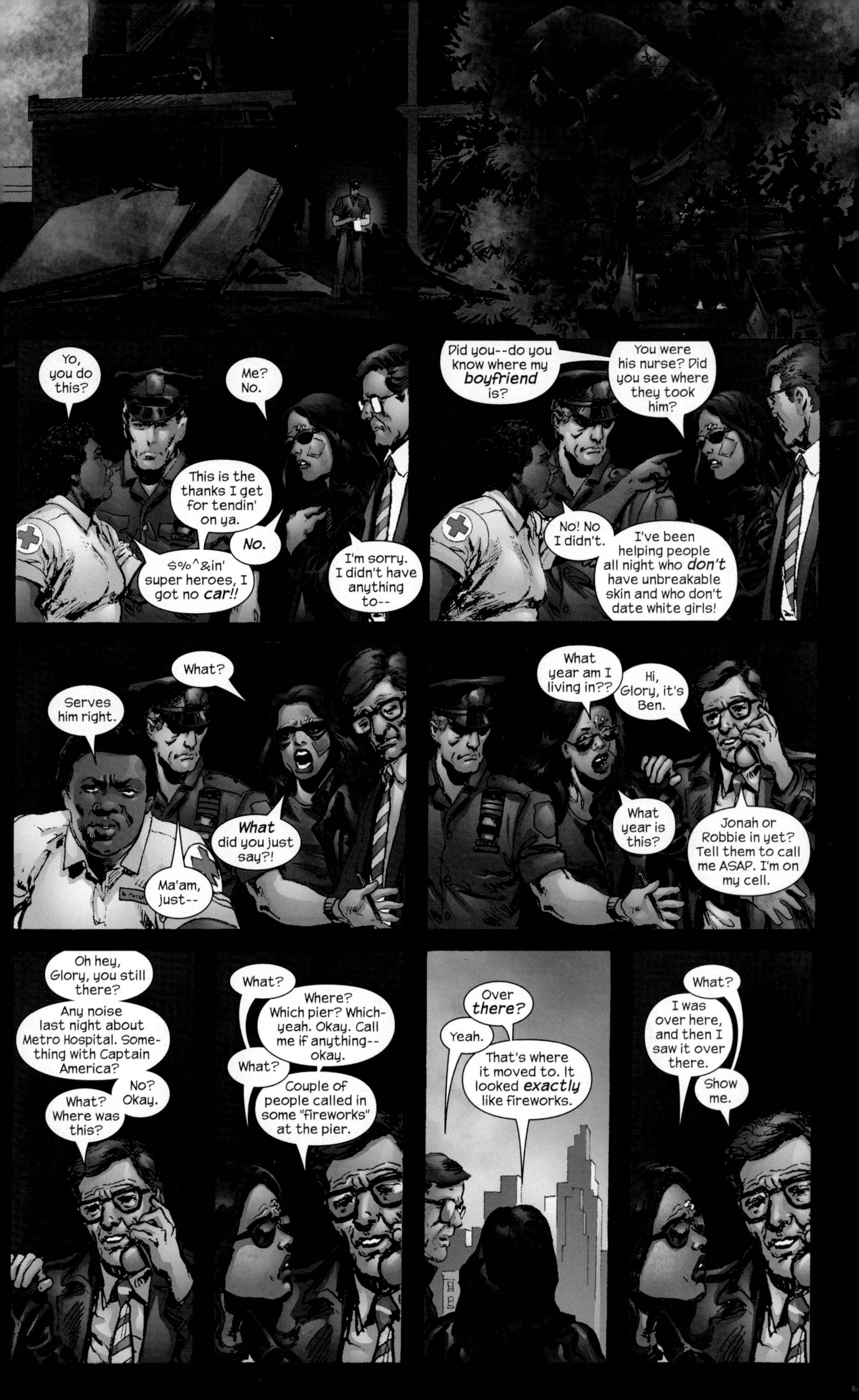
Yo, you do this?
Me? No.
This is the thanks I get for tendin' on ya.
No.
$%^&in' super heroes, I got no car!!
I'm sorry. I didn't have anything to--
Did you--do you know where my boyfriend is?
You were his nurse? Did you see where they took him?
No! No I didn't.
I've been helping people all night who don't have unbreakable skin and who don't date white girls!
Serves him right.
What?
What did you just say?!
Ma'am, just--
What year am I living in??
Hi, Glory, it's Ben.
What year is this?
Jonah or Robbie in yet? Tell them to call me ASAP. I'm on my cell.
Oh hey, Glory, you still there?
Any noise last night about Metro Hospital. Something with Captain America?
No? Okay.
What? Where was this?
What?
Where? Which pier? Which- yeah. Okay. Call me if anything-- okay.
What?
Couple of people called in some "fireworks" at the pier.
Over there?
Yeah.
That's where it moved to. It looked exactly like fireworks.
What?
I was over here, and then I saw it over there.
Show me.

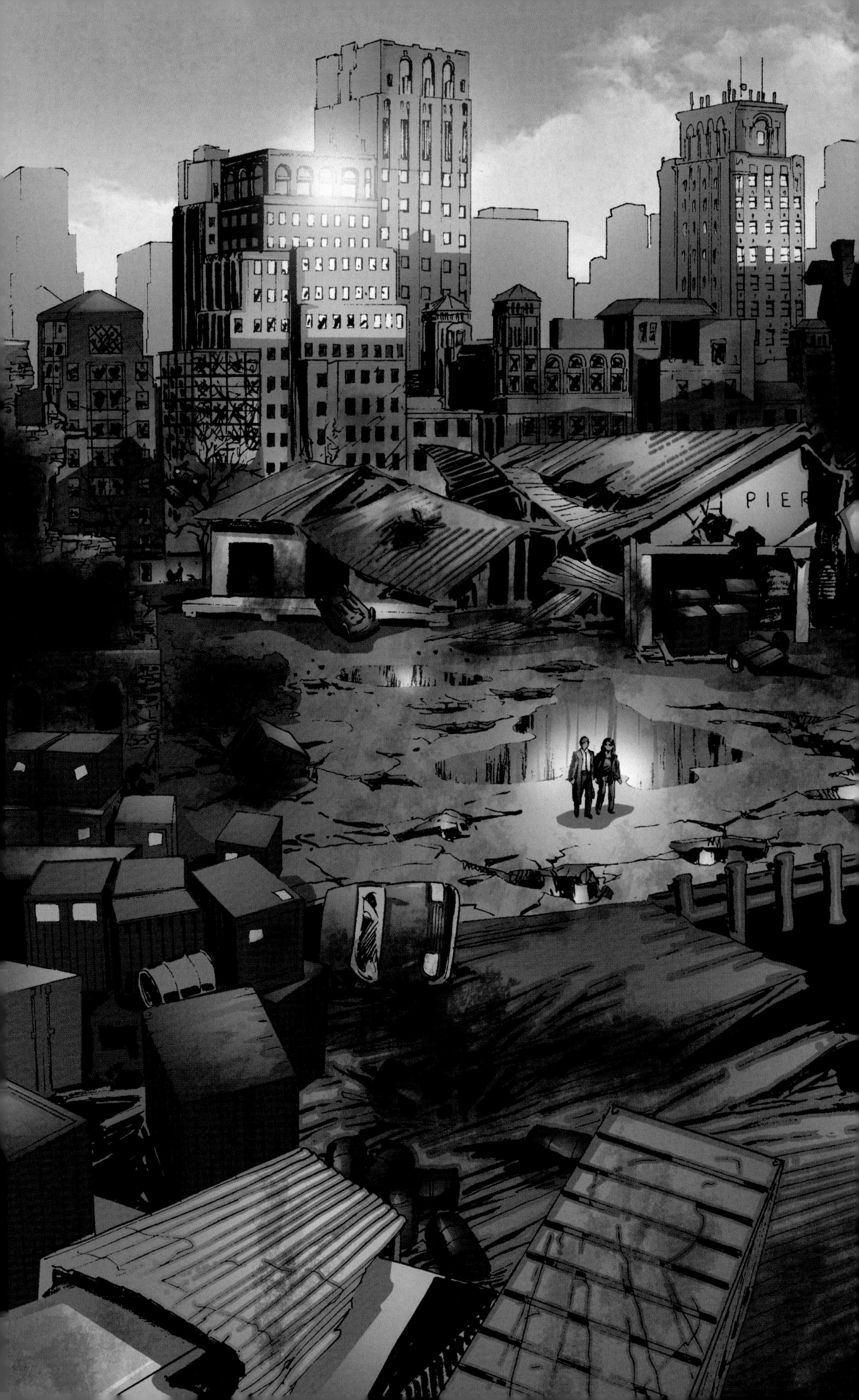
PIER

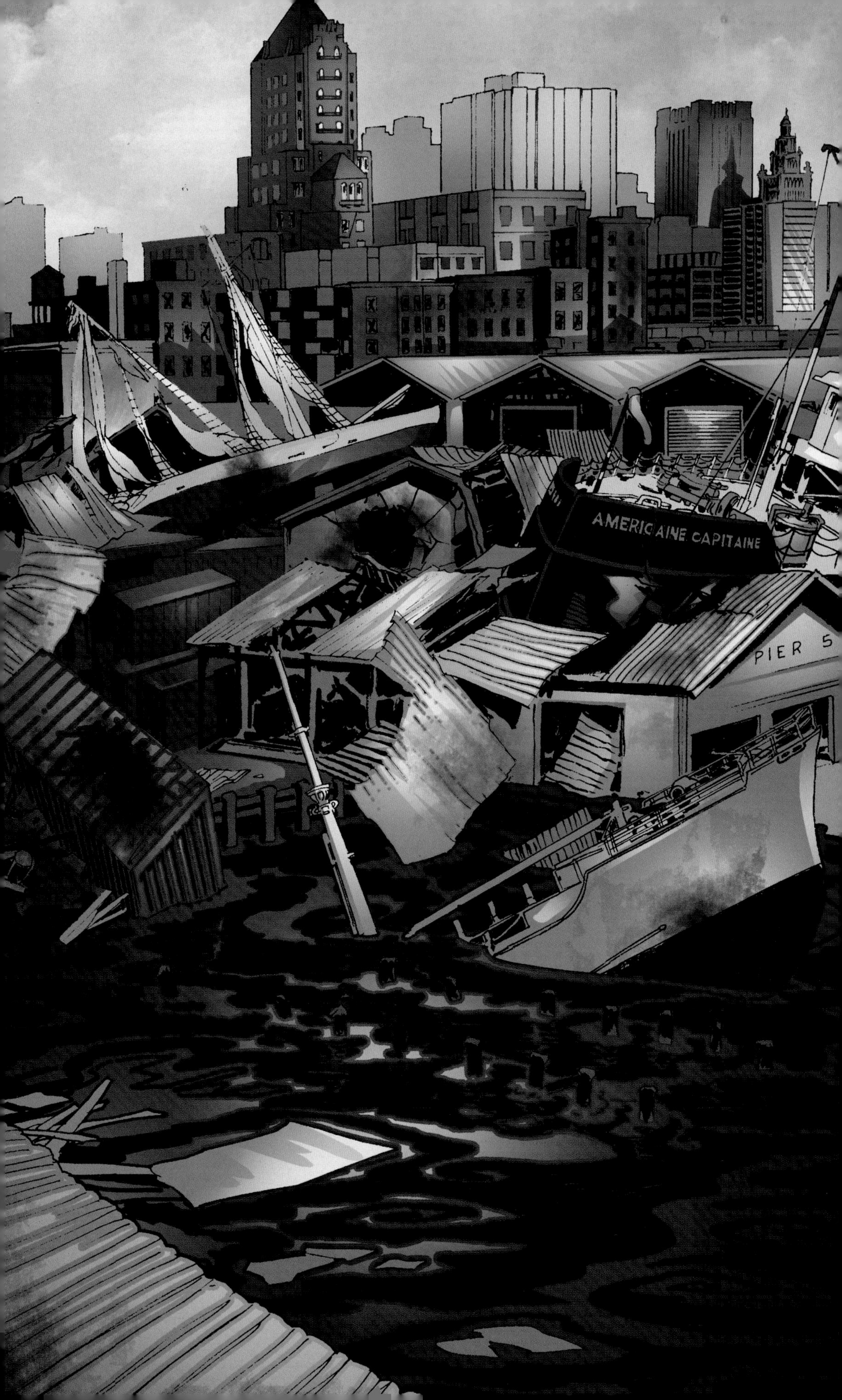
AMERICAINE CAPITAINE
PIER 5

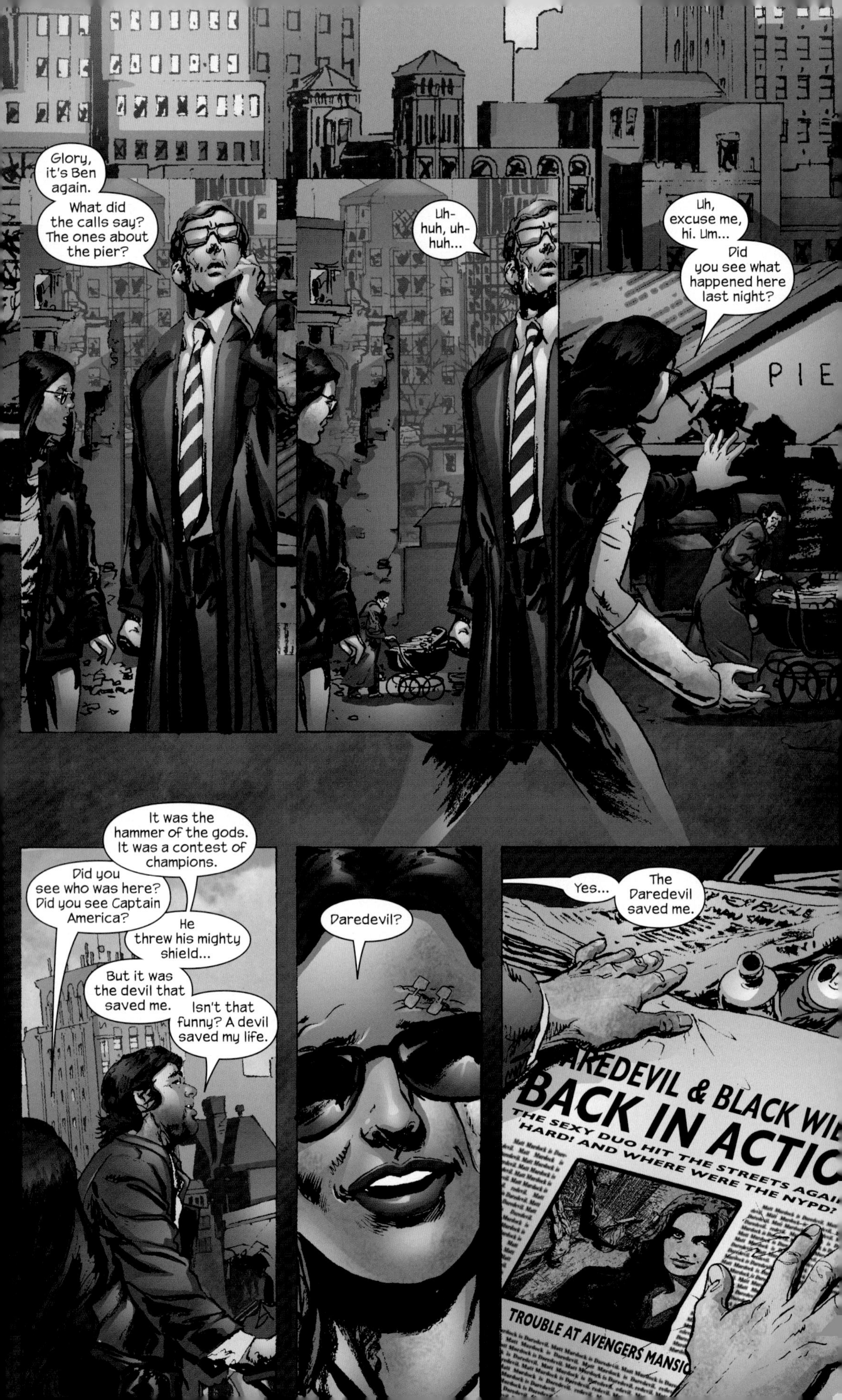

Glory, it's Ben again.
What did the calls say? The ones about the pier?
Uh-huh, uh-huh...
Uh, excuse me, hi. Um...
Did you see what happened here last night?
PIE
Did you see who was here? Did you see Captain America?
It was the hammer of the gods. It was a contest of champions.
He threw his mighty shield...
But it was the devil that saved me.
Isn't that funny? A devil saved my life.
Daredevil?
Yes...
The Daredevil saved me.
AREDEVIL & BLACK WI
BACK IN ACTIC
THE SEXY DUO HIT THE STREETS AGAI
HARD! AND WHERE WERE THE NYPD?
TROUBLE AT AVENGERS MANSIO

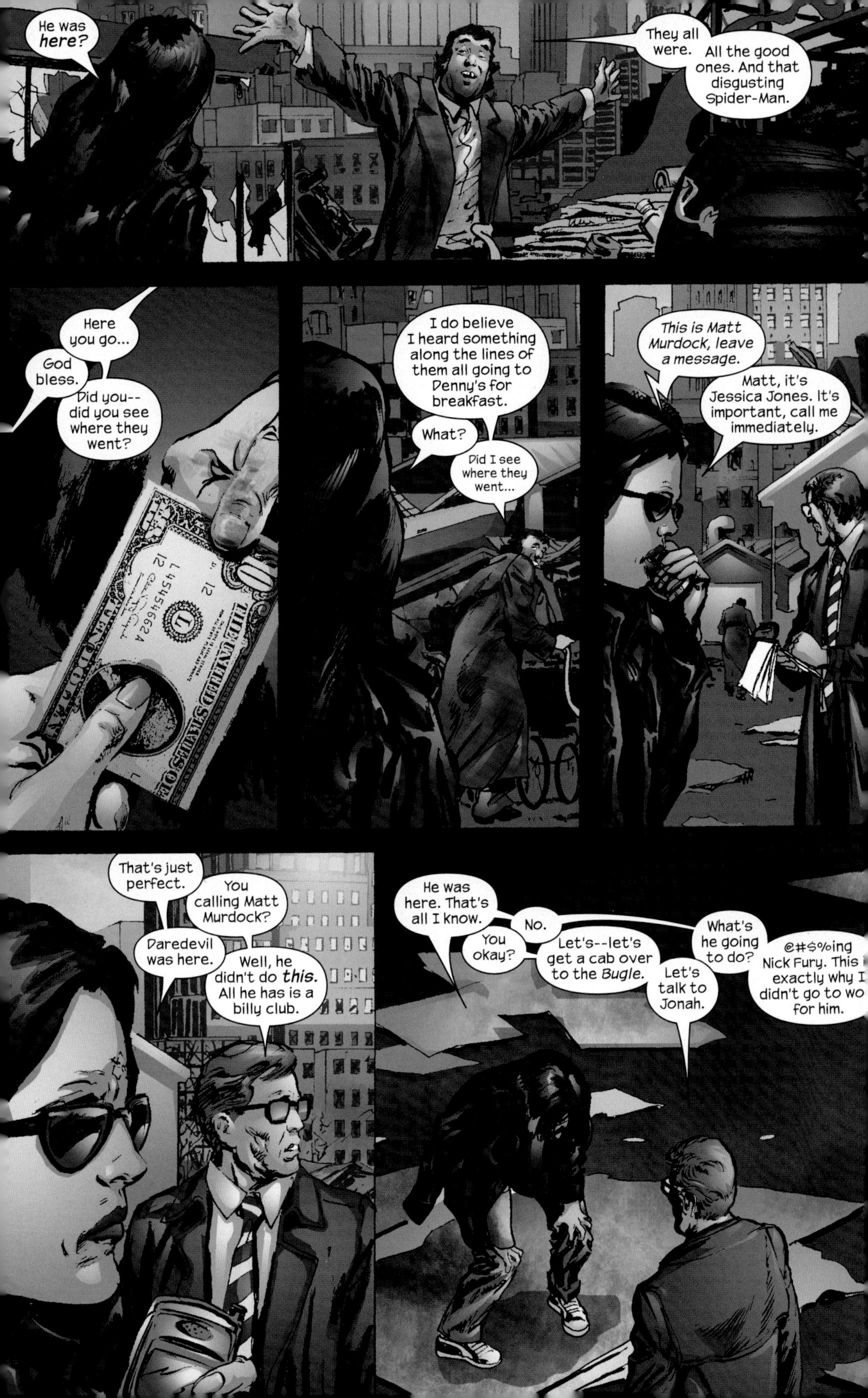

He was *here*?
They all were.
All the good ones. And that disgusting Spider-Man.
Here you go...
God bless.
Did you-- did you see where they went?
I do believe I heard something along the lines of them all going to Denny's for breakfast.
What?
Did I see where they went...
This is Matt Murdock, leave a message.
Matt, it's Jessica Jones. It's important, call me immediately.
That's just perfect.
You calling Matt Murdock?
Daredevil was here.
Well, he didn't do **this.** All he has is a billy club.
He was here. That's all I know.
No.
You okay?
Let's--let's get a cab over to the *Bugle*.
What's he going to do?
Let's talk to Jonah.
@#$%ing Nick Fury. This exactly why I didn't go to wo for him.

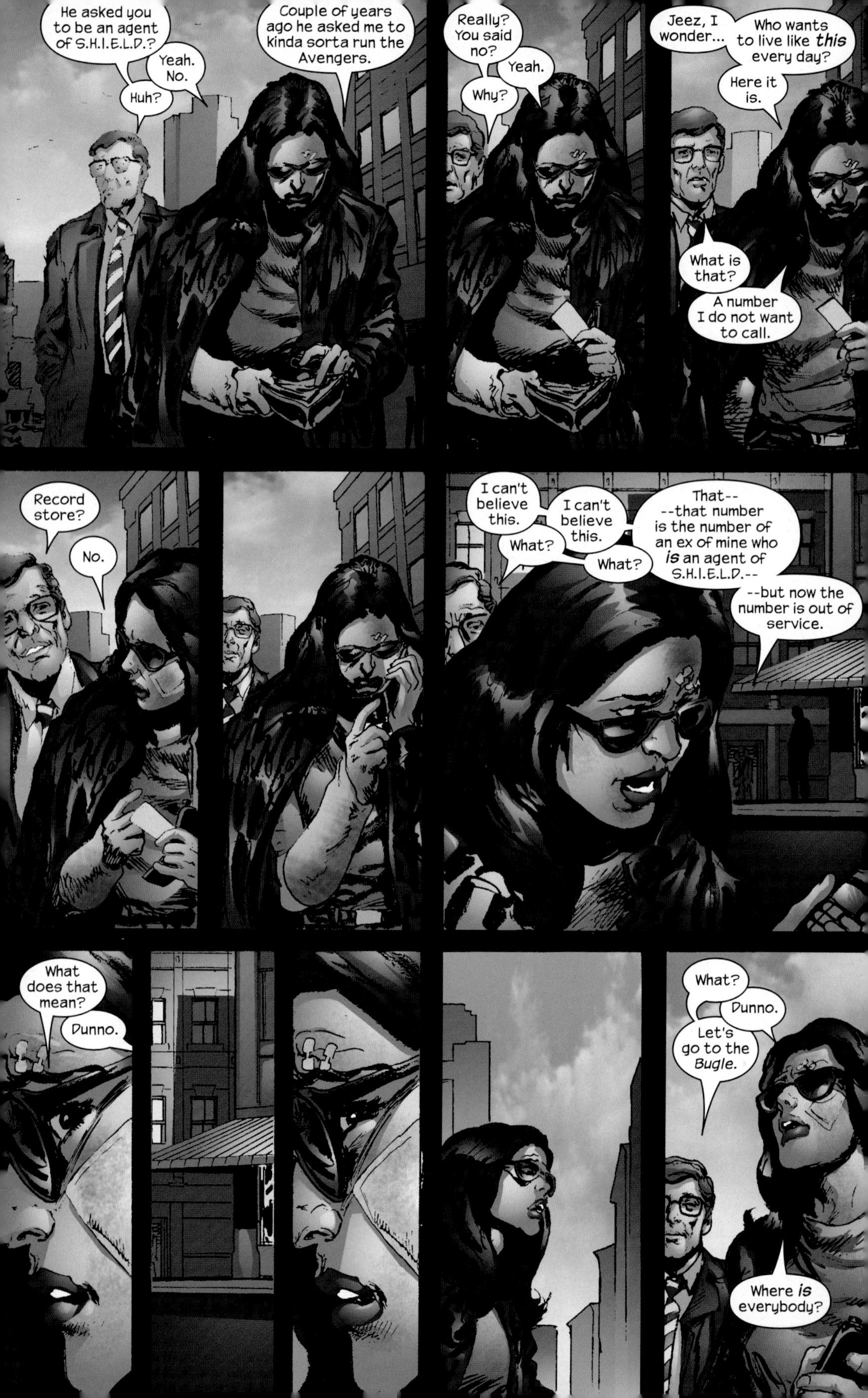
He asked you to be an agent of S.H.I.E.L.D.?
Huh?
Yeah. No.
Couple of years ago he asked me to kinda sorta run the Avengers.
Really? You said no?
Why?
Yeah.
Jeez, I wonder...
Who wants to live like *this* every day?
Here it is.
What is that?
A number I do not want to call.
Record store?
No.
I can't believe this.
What?
I can't believe this.
What?
That-- --that number is the number of an ex of mine who *is* an agent of S.H.I.E.L.D.--
--but now the number is out of service.
What does that mean?
Dunno.
What?
Dunno.
Let's go to the *Bugle*.
Where *is* everybody?

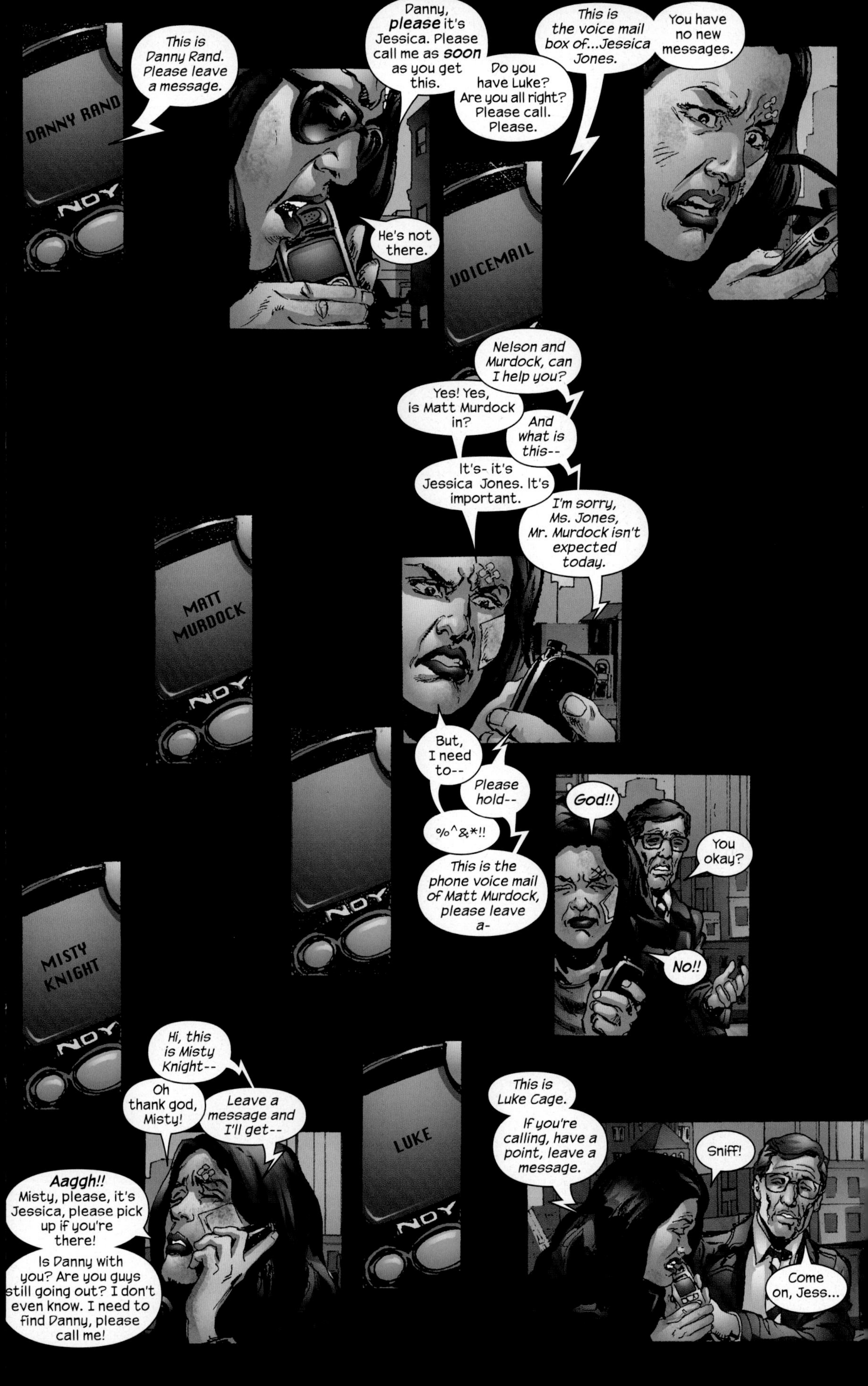

DANNY RAND
NOY
This is Danny Rand. Please leave a message.
Danny, please it's Jessica. Please call me as soon as you get this.
He's not there.
Do you have Luke? Are you all right? Please call. Please.
VOICEMAIL
This is the voice mail box of...Jessica Jones.
You have no new messages.
Nelson and Murdock, can I help you?
Yes! Yes, is Matt Murdock in?
And what is this--
It's- it's Jessica Jones. It's important.
I'm sorry, Ms. Jones, Mr. Murdock isn't expected today.
MATT MURDOCK
NOY
But, I need to--
Please hold--
%^&*!!
This is the phone voice mail of Matt Murdock, please leave a-
NOY
God!!
You okay?
No!!
MISTY KNIGHT
NOY
Hi, this is Misty Knight--
Oh thank god, Misty!
Leave a message and I'll get--
Aagggh!! Misty, please, it's Jessica, please pick up if you're there!
Is Danny with you? Are you guys still going out? I don't even know. I need to find Danny, please call me!
LUKE
NOY
This is Luke Cage.
If you're calling, have a point, leave a message.
Sniff!
Come on, Jess...

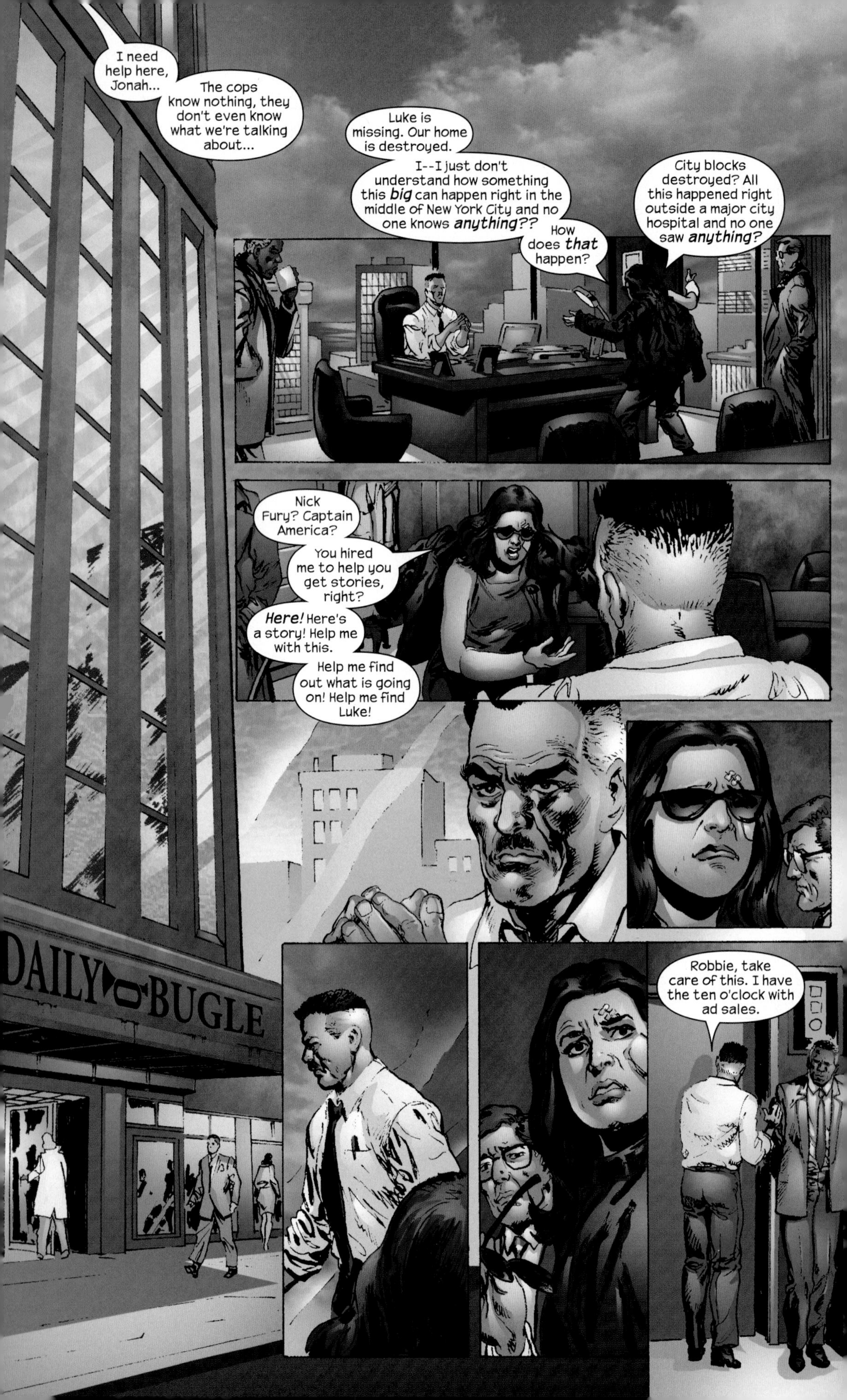
I need help here, Jonah...
The cops know nothing, they don't even know what we're talking about...
Luke is missing. Our home is destroyed.
I--I just don't understand how something this *big* can happen right in the middle of New York City and no one knows *anything*??
How does *that* happen?
City blocks destroyed? All this happened right outside a major city hospital and no one saw *anything*?
Nick Fury? Captain America?
You hired me to help you get stories, right?
Here! Here's a story! Help me with this.
Help me find out what is going on! Help me find Luke!
DAILY BUGLE
Robbie, take care of this. I have the ten o'clock with ad sales.

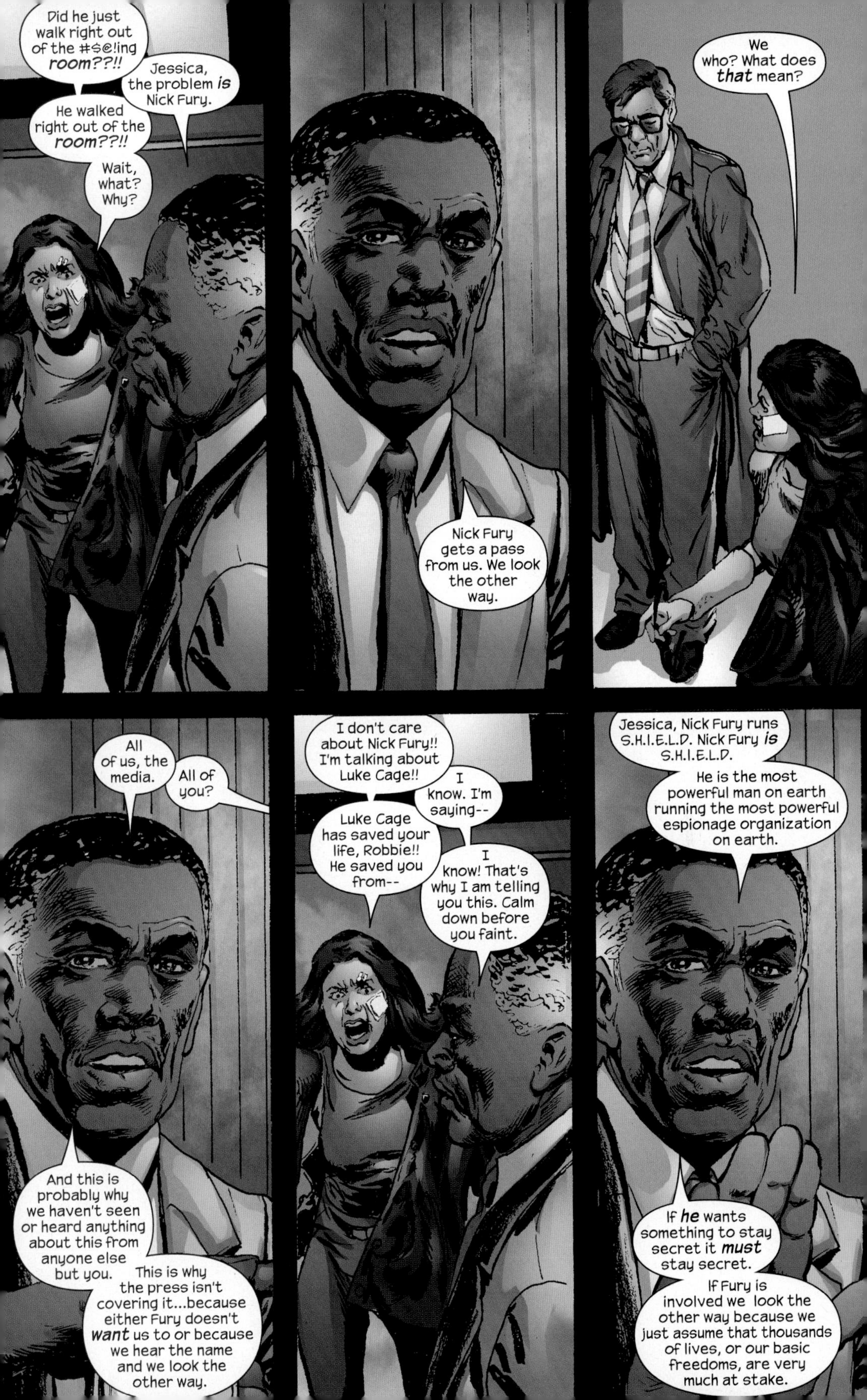
Did he just walk right out of the #$@!ing room??!!
Jessica, the problem is Nick Fury.
He walked right out of the room??!!
Wait, what? Why?
Nick Fury gets a pass from us. We look the other way.
We who? What does that mean?
All of us, the media.
All of you?
And this is probably why we haven't seen or heard anything about this from anyone else but you.
This is why the press isn't covering it...because either Fury doesn't want us to or because we hear the name and we look the other way.
I don't care about Nick Fury!! I'm talking about Luke Cage!!
I know. I'm saying--
Luke Cage has saved your life, Robbie!! He saved you from--
I know! That's why I am telling you this. Calm down before you faint.
Jessica, Nick Fury runs S.H.I.E.L.D. Nick Fury is S.H.I.E.L.D.
He is the most powerful man on earth running the most powerful espionage organization on earth.
If he wants something to stay secret it must stay secret.
If Fury is involved we look the other way because we just assume that thousands of lives, or our basic freedoms, are very much at stake.

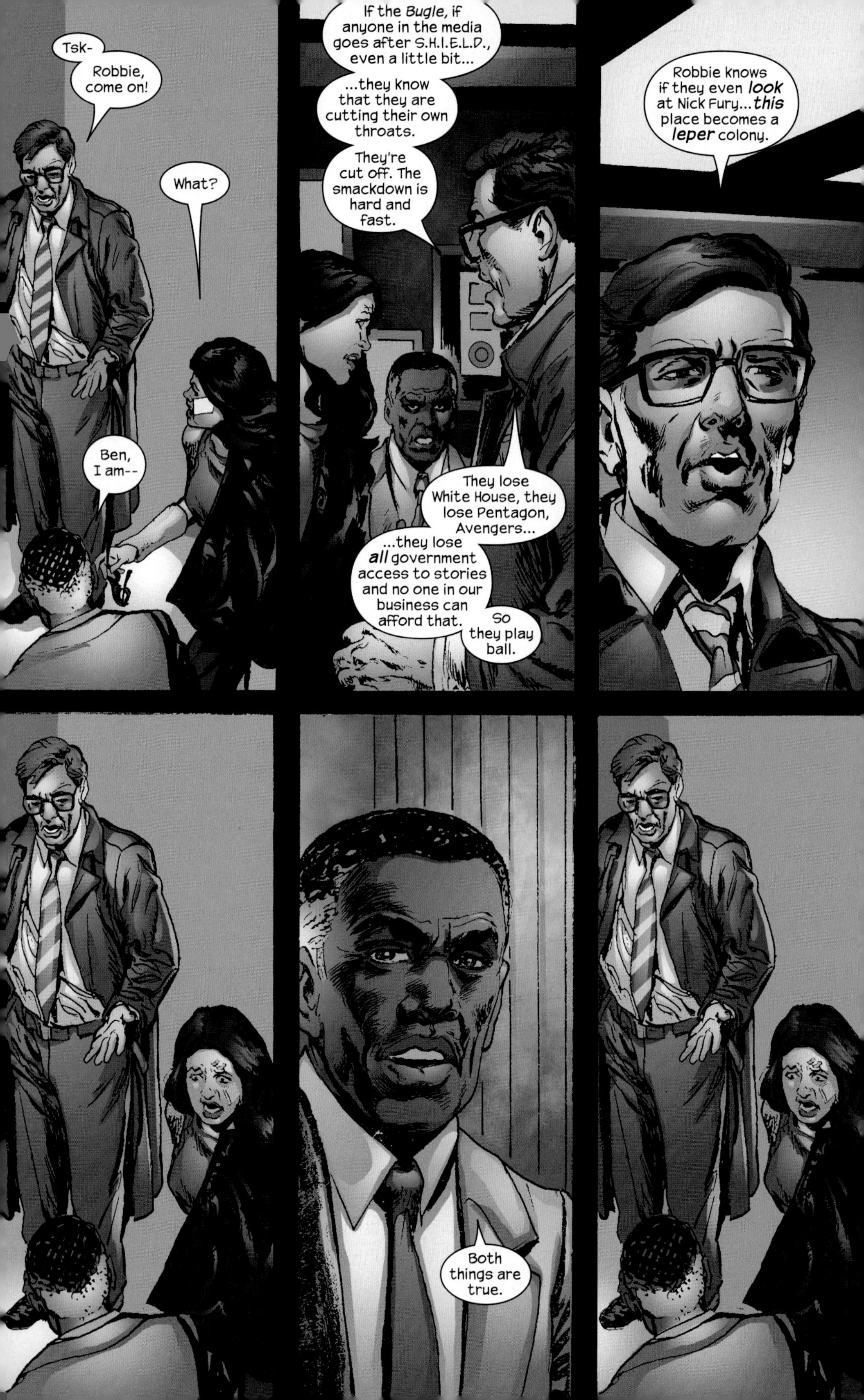
Tsk-
Robbie, come on!
What?
Ben, I am--
If the Bugle, if anyone in the media goes after S.H.I.E.L.D., even a little bit...
...they know that they are cutting their own throats.
They're cut off. The smackdown is hard and fast.
They lose White House, they lose Pentagon, Avengers...
...they lose all government access to stories and no one in our business can afford that.
So they play ball.
Robbie knows if they even look at Nick Fury...this place becomes a leper colony.
Both things are true.

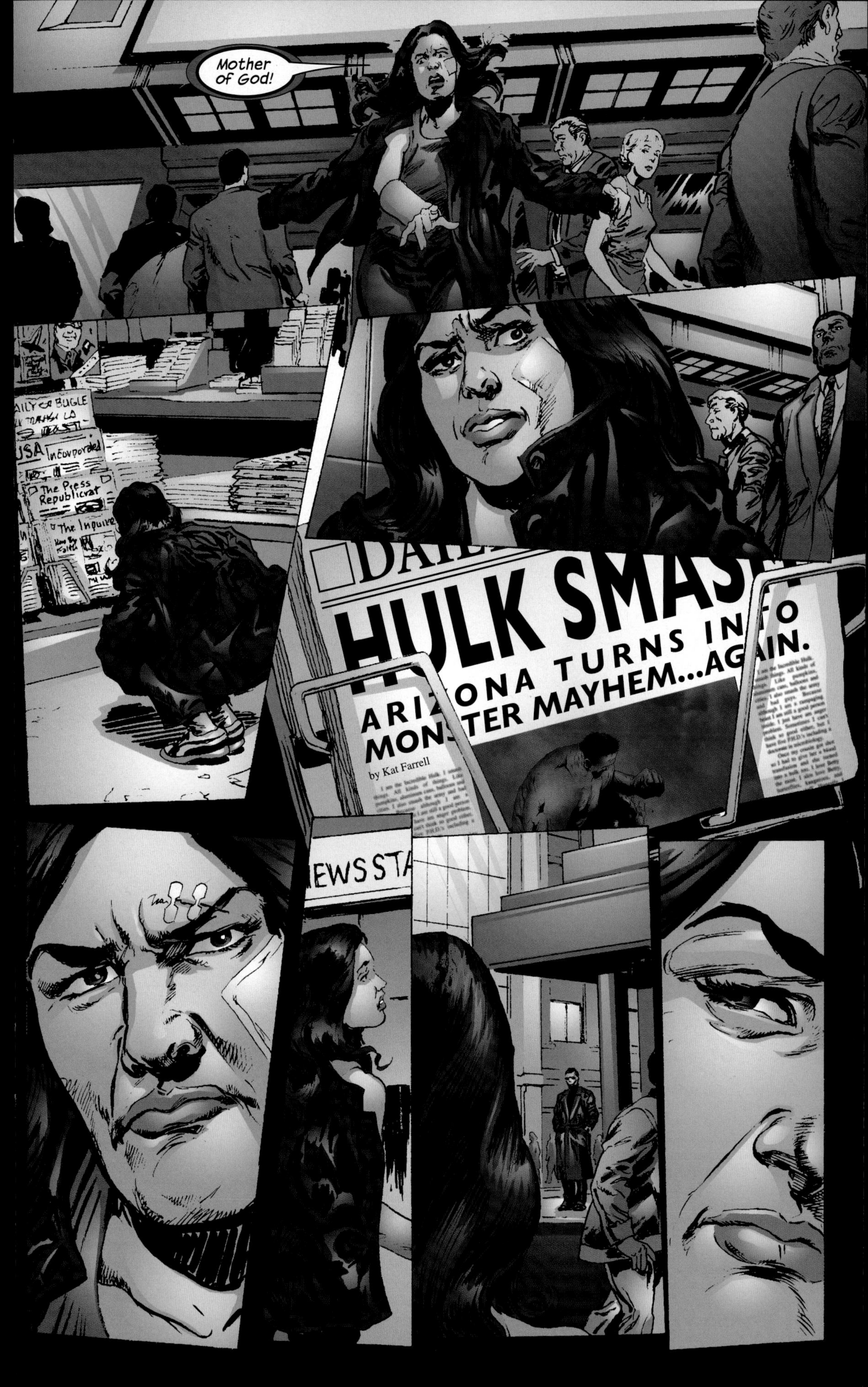
Mother of God!
DAILY BUGLE
The Press Republicrat
The Inquire
HULK SMAS
ARIZONA TURNS INTO MONSTER MAYHEM...AGAIN.
by Kat Farrell
NEWS STA

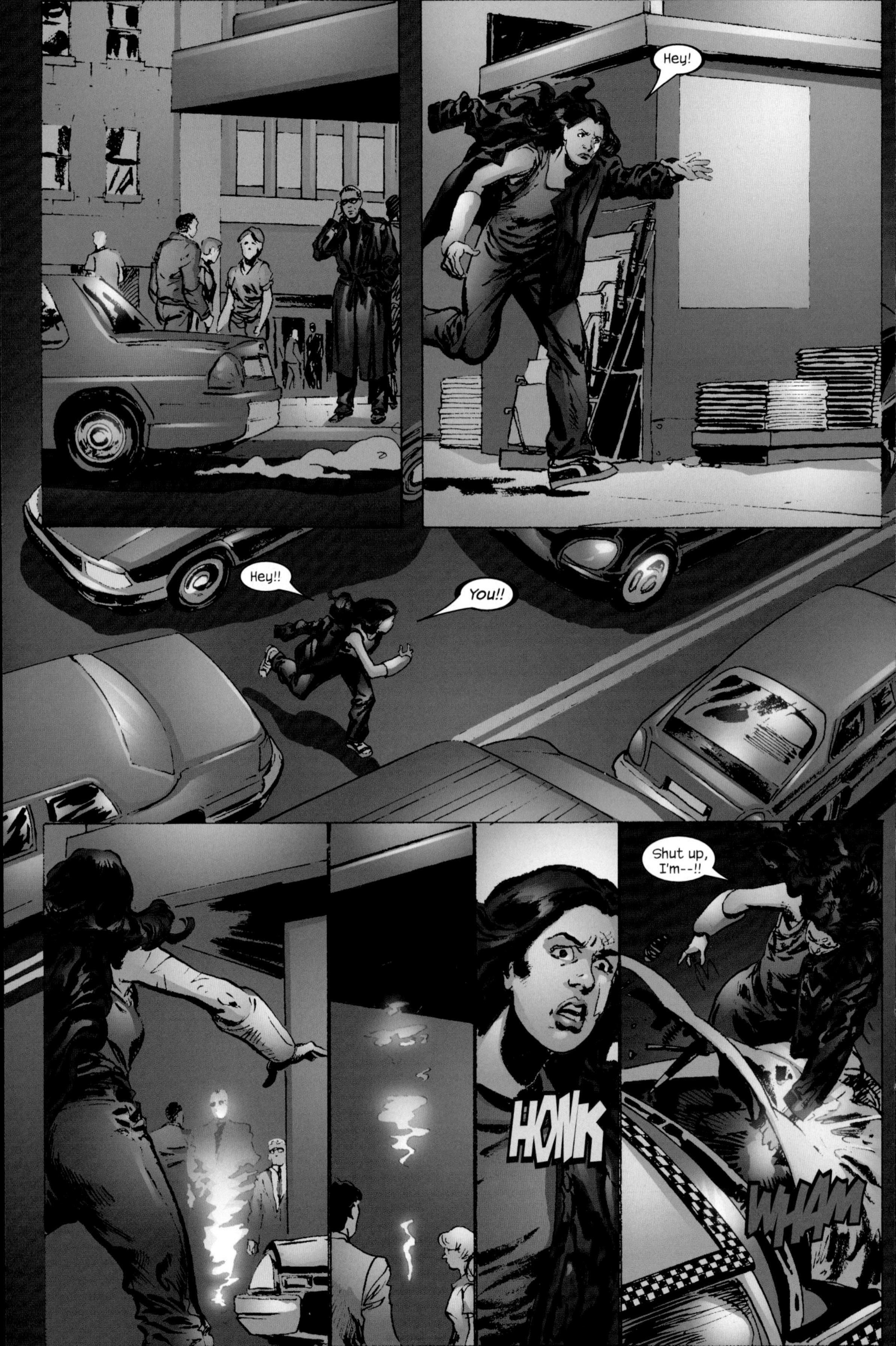
Hey!
Hey!!
You!!
HONK
Shut up, I'm--!!
WHAM

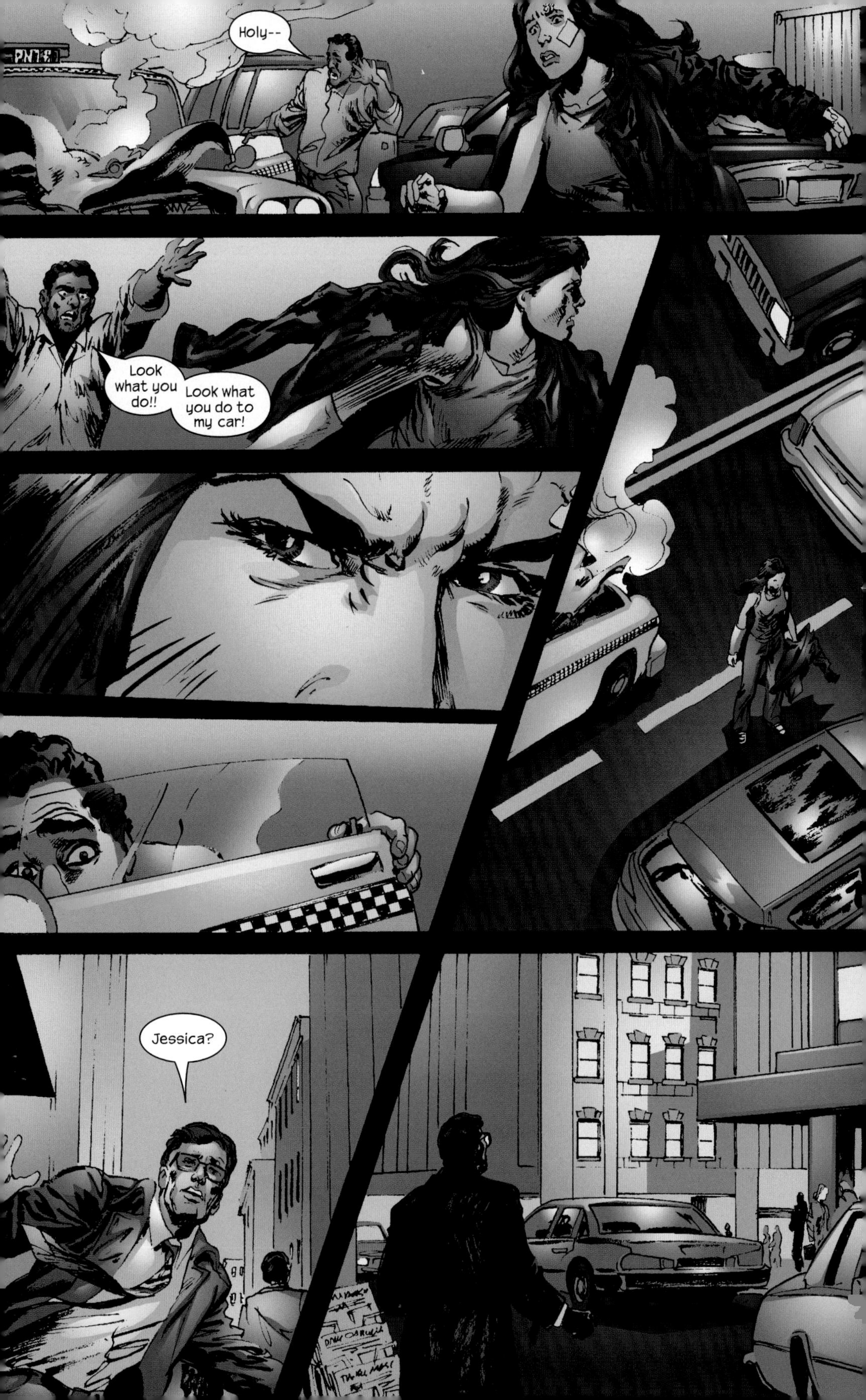
Holy--
Look what you do!!
Look what you do to my car!
Jessica?

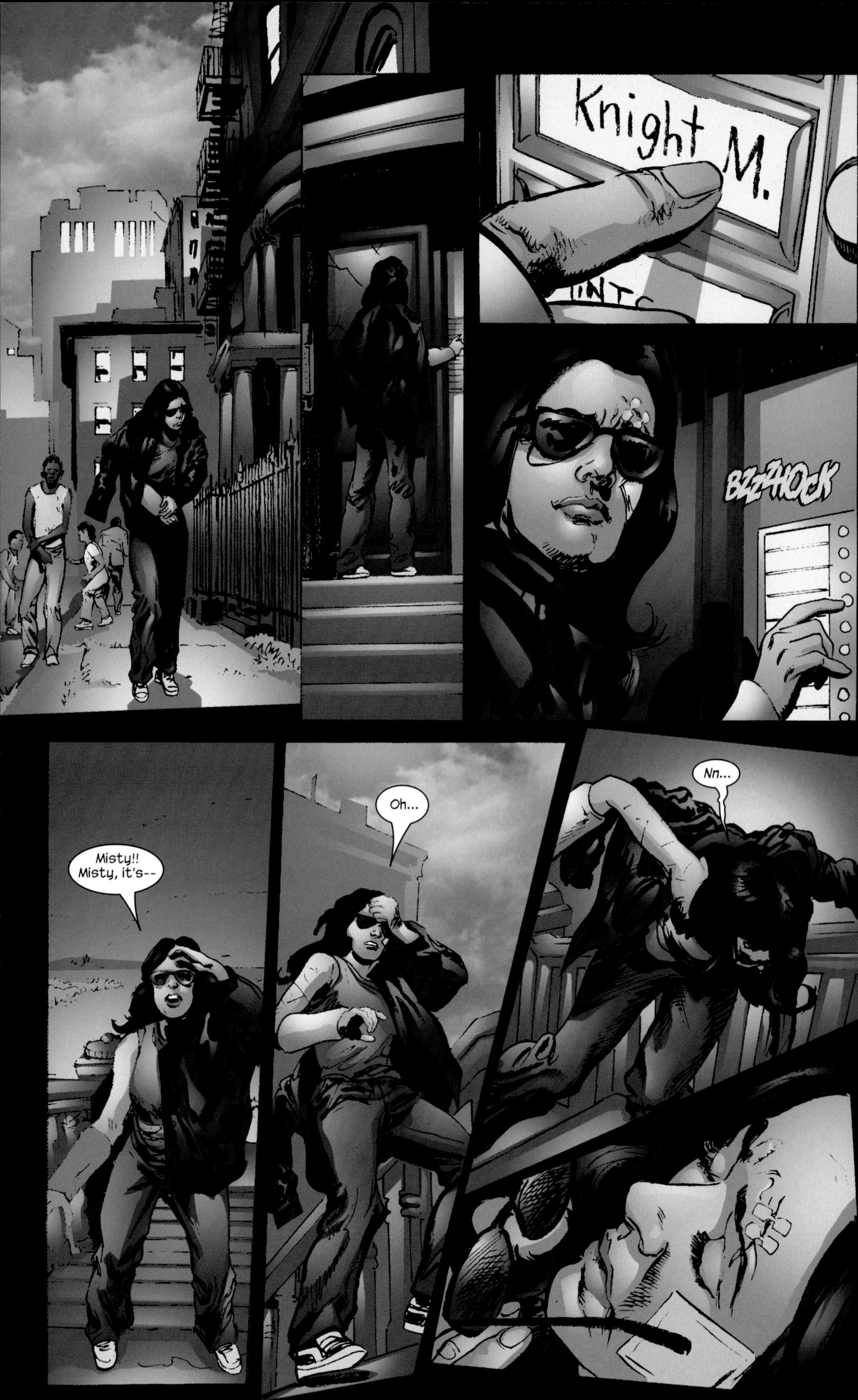
Knight M.
BZZZHOCK
Misty!!
Misty, it's--
Oh...
Nn...

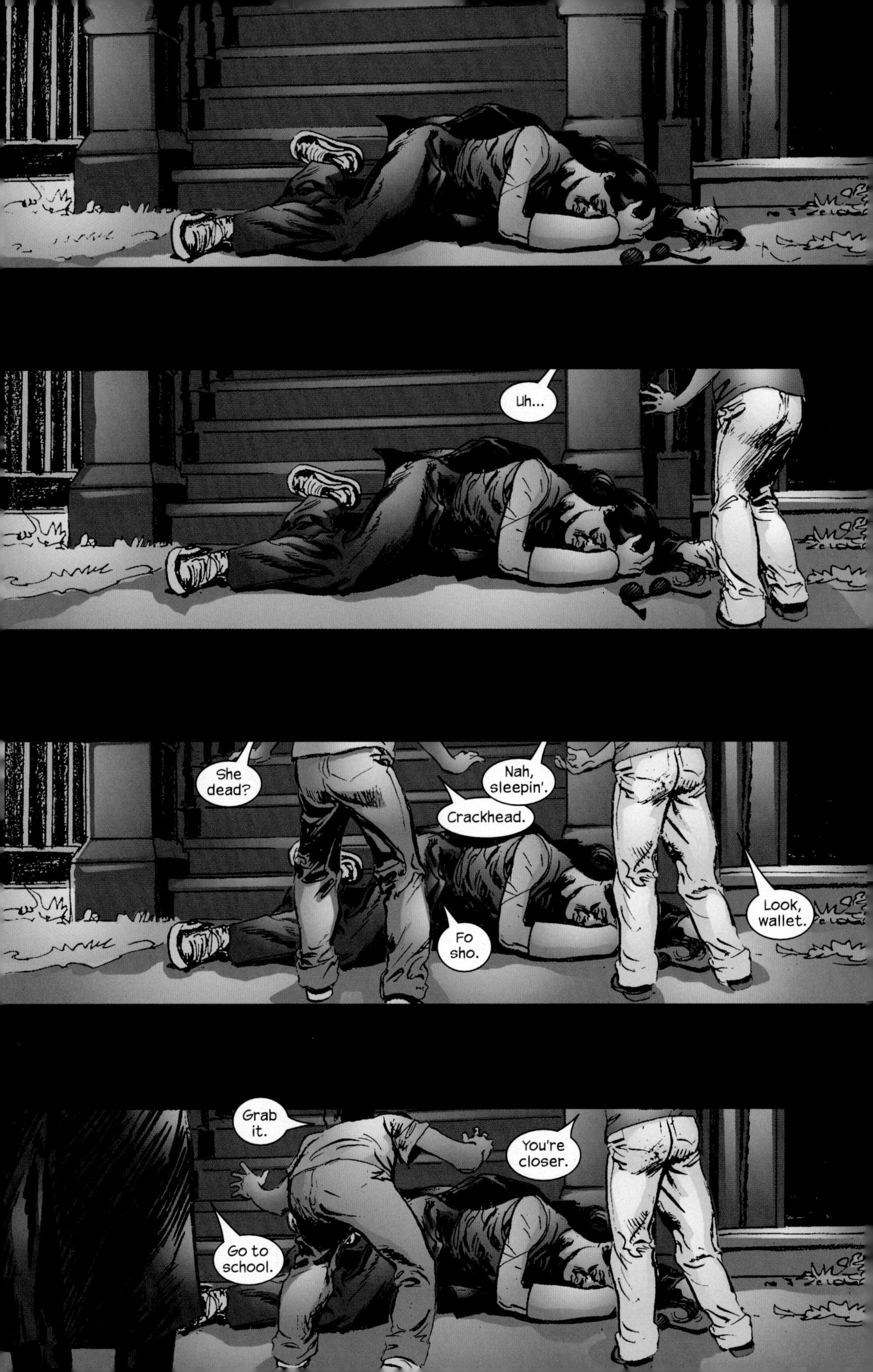
Uh...
She dead?
Nah, sleepin'.
Crackhead.
Fo sho.
Look, wallet.
Grab it.
You're closer.
Go to school.

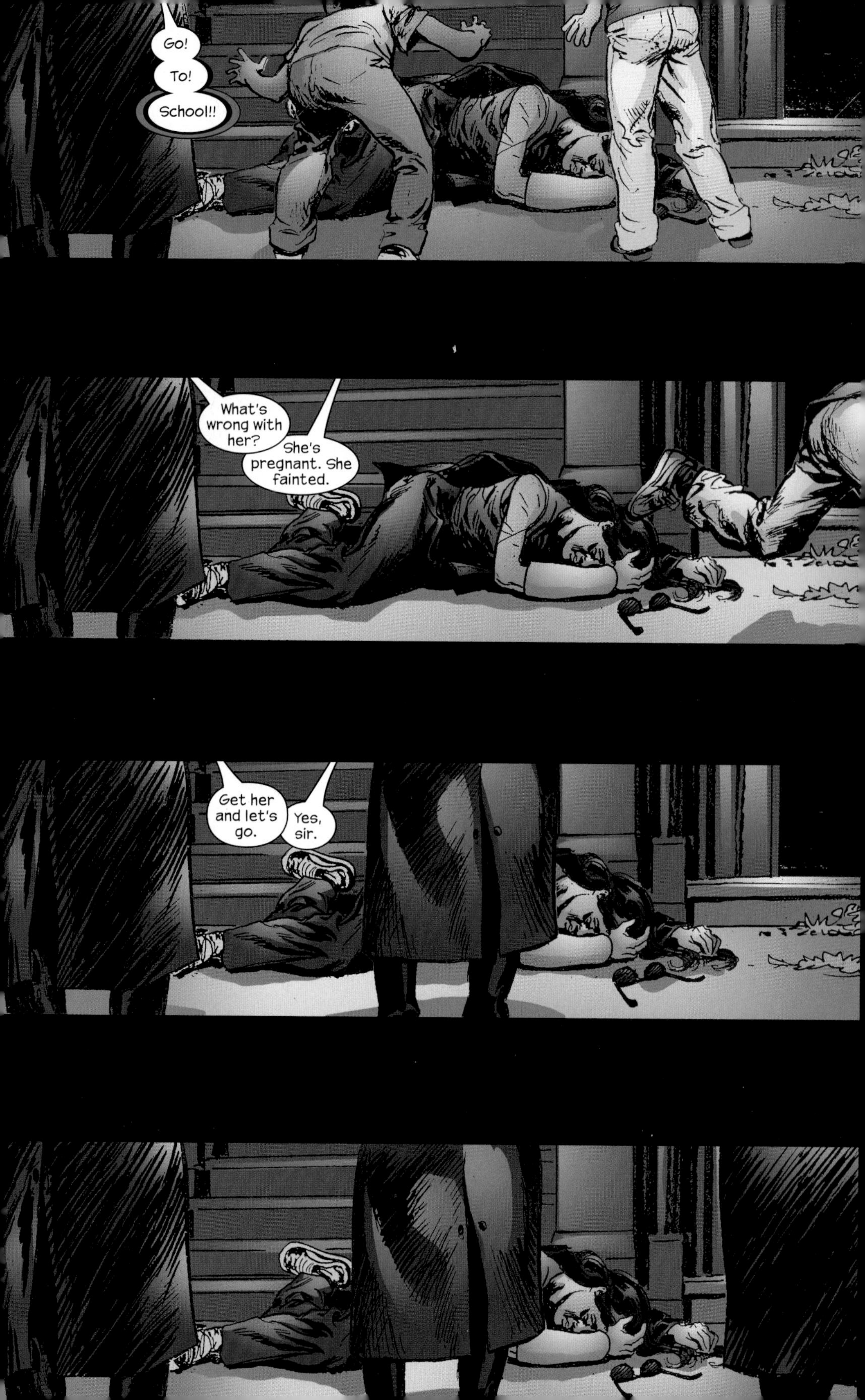
Go!
To!
School!!
What's wrong with her?
She's pregnant. She fainted.
Get her and let's go.
Yes, sir.

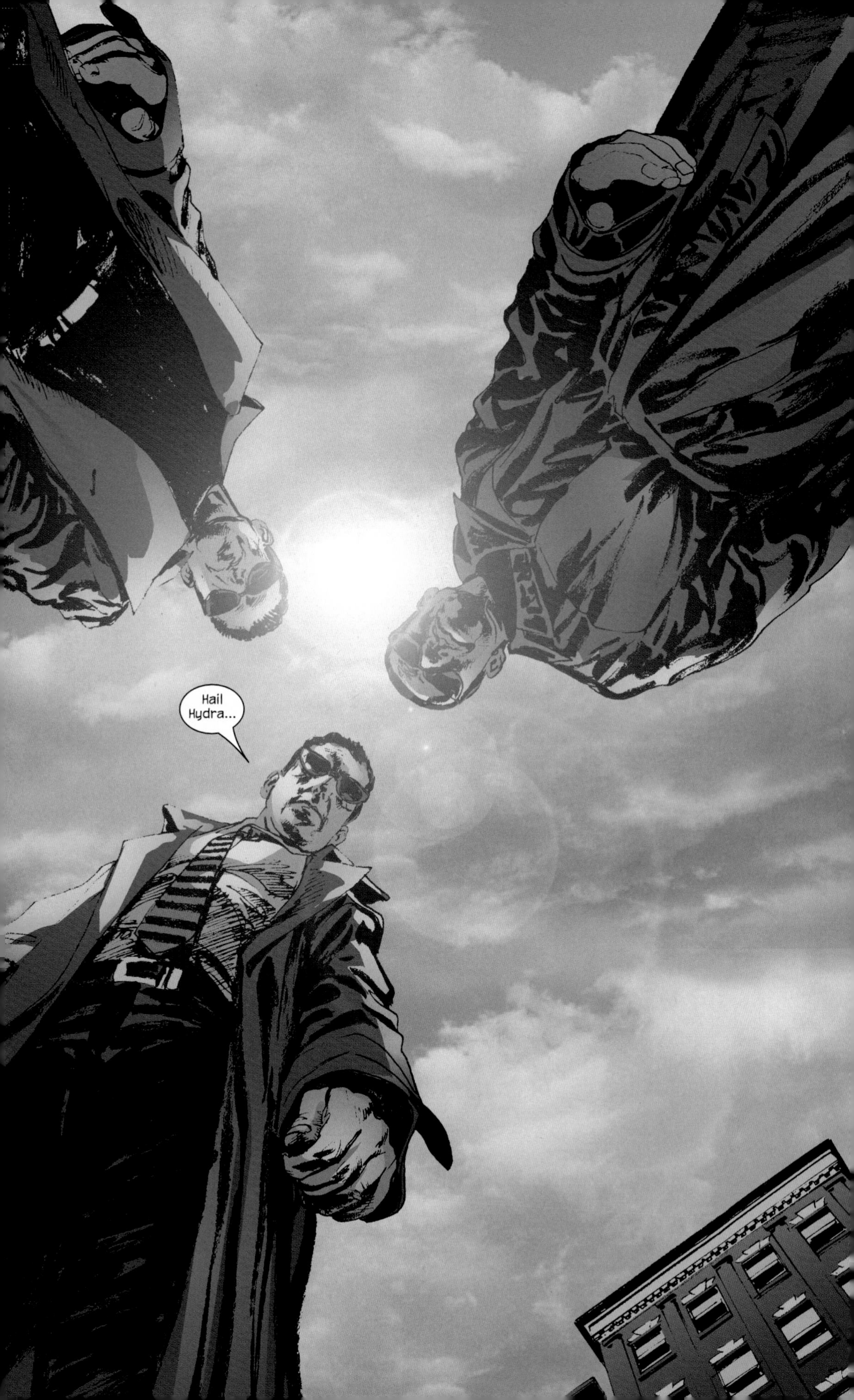
Hail Hydra...

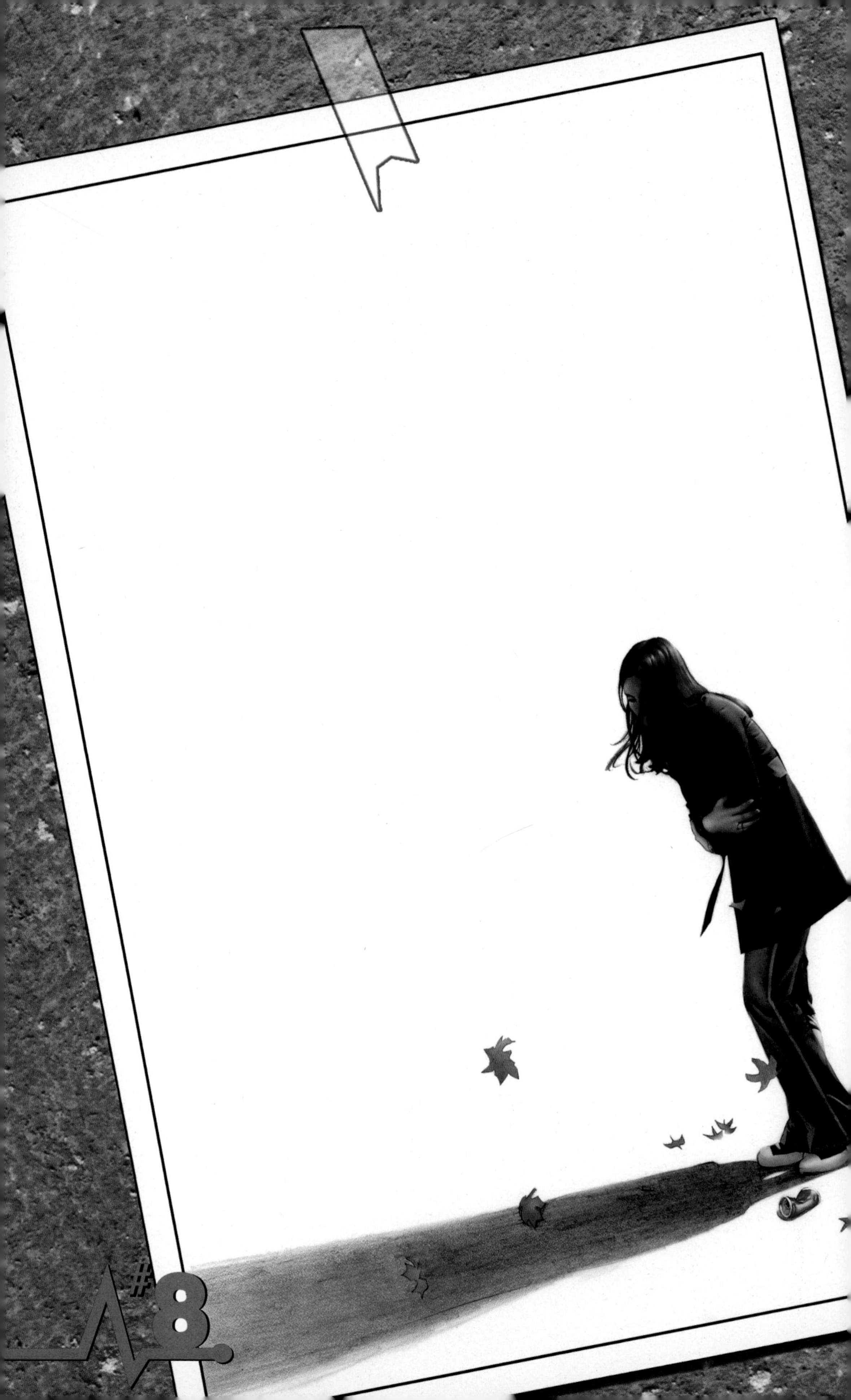
#8

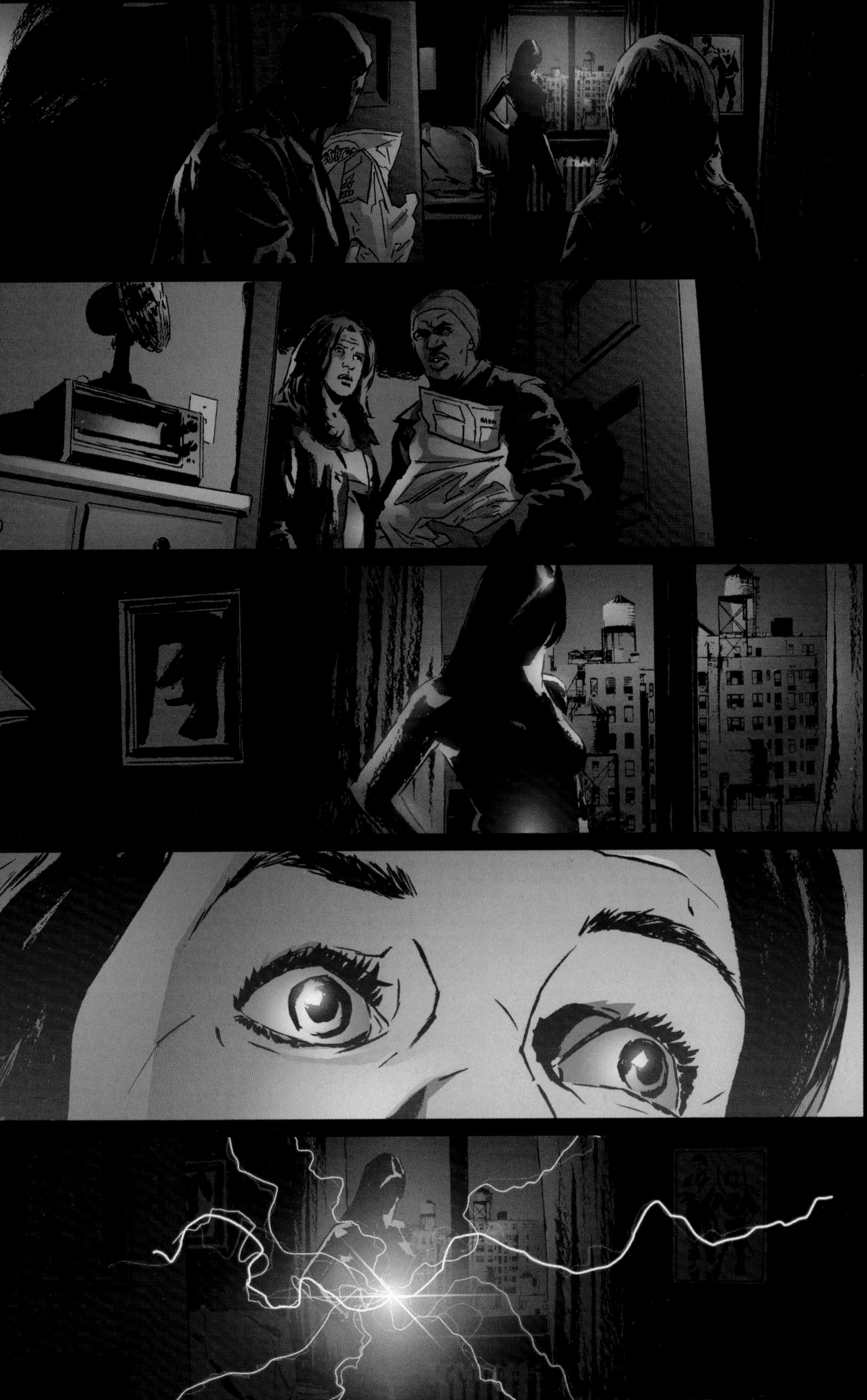

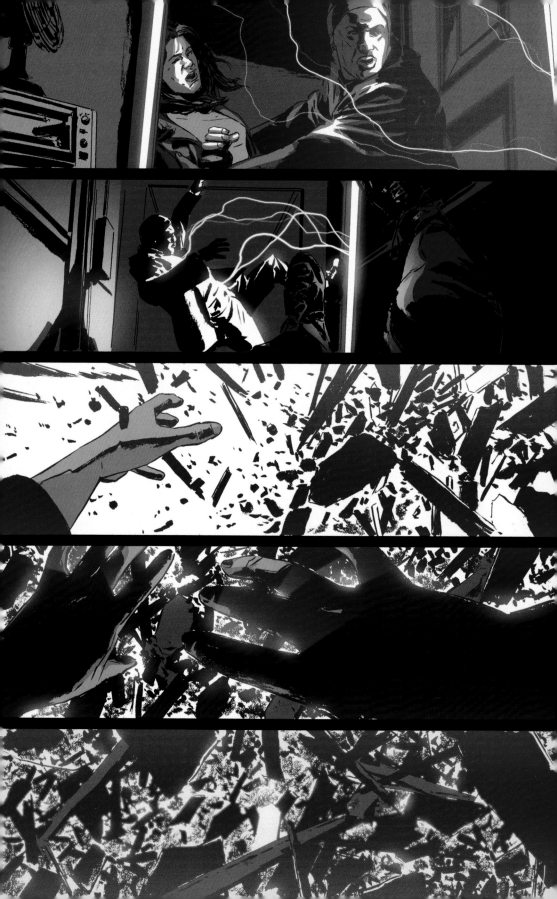

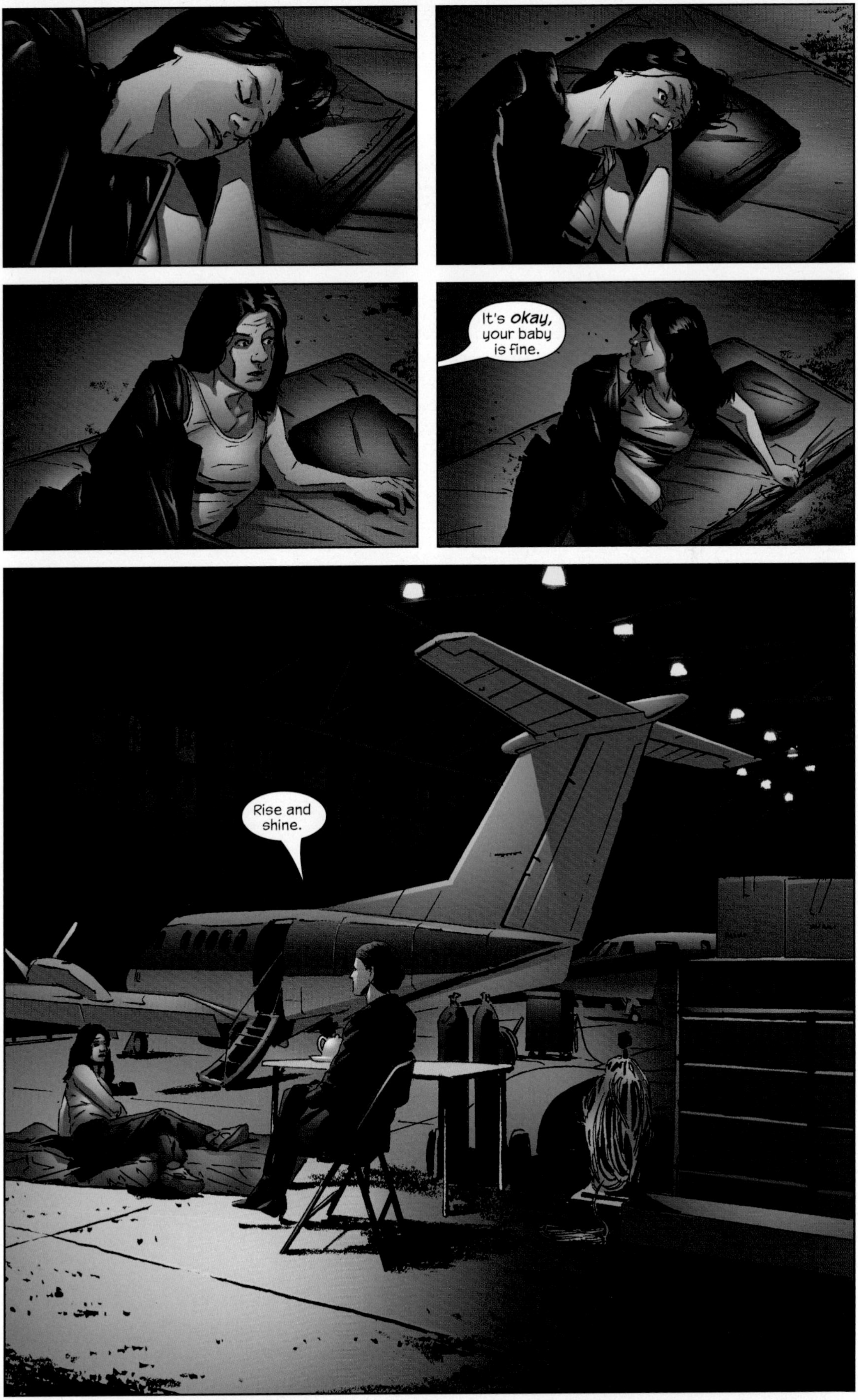
It's okay, your baby is fine.
Rise and shine.

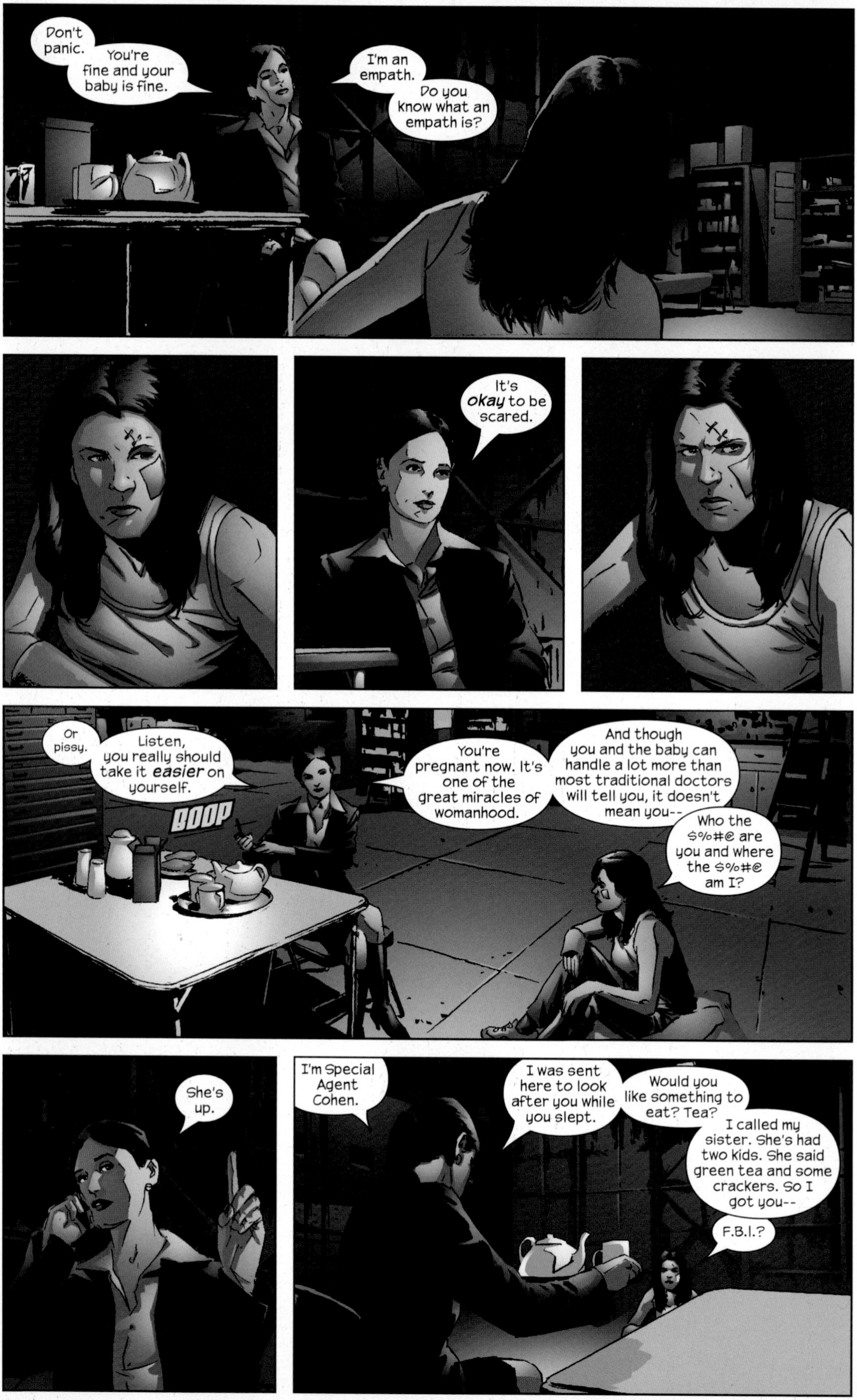
Don't panic.
You're fine and your baby is fine.
I'm an empath.
Do you know what an empath is?
It's okay to be scared.
Or pissy.
Listen, you really should take it easier on yourself.
BOOP
You're pregnant now. It's one of the great miracles of womanhood.
And though you and the baby can handle a lot more than most traditional doctors will tell you, it doesn't mean you--
Who the $%#@ are you and where the $%#@ am I?
She's up.
I'm Special Agent Cohen.
I was sent here to look after you while you slept.
Would you like something to eat? Tea?
I called my sister. She's had two kids. She said green tea and some crackers. So I got you--
F.B.I.?

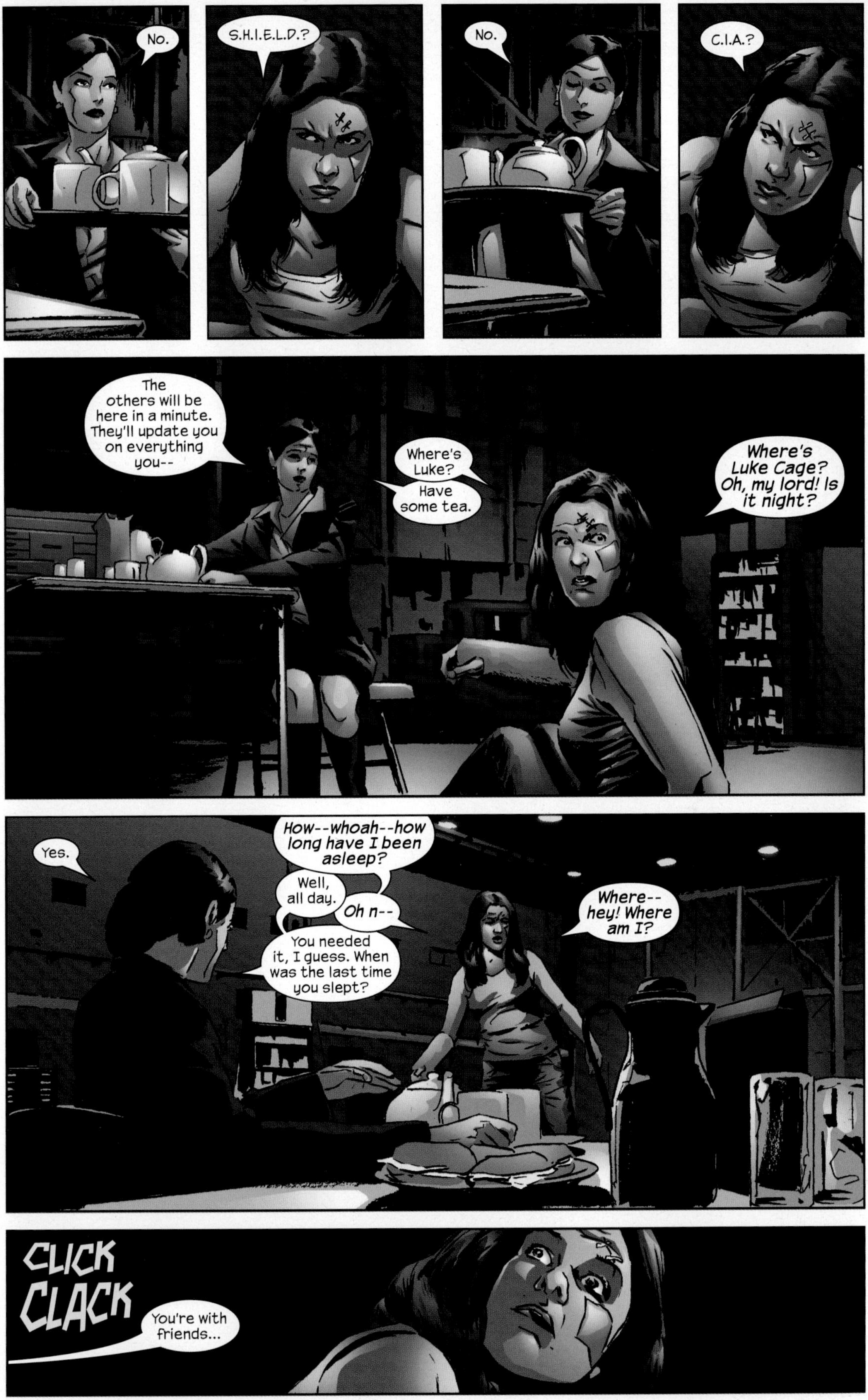
No.
S.H.I.E.L.D.?
No.
C.I.A.?
The others will be here in a minute. They'll update you on everything you--
Where's Luke?
Have some tea.
Where's Luke Cage? Oh, my lord! Is it night?
Yes.
How--whoah--how long have I been asleep?
Well, all day.
Oh n--
You needed it, I guess. When was the last time you slept?
Where-- hey! Where am I?
CLICK
CLACK
You're with friends...

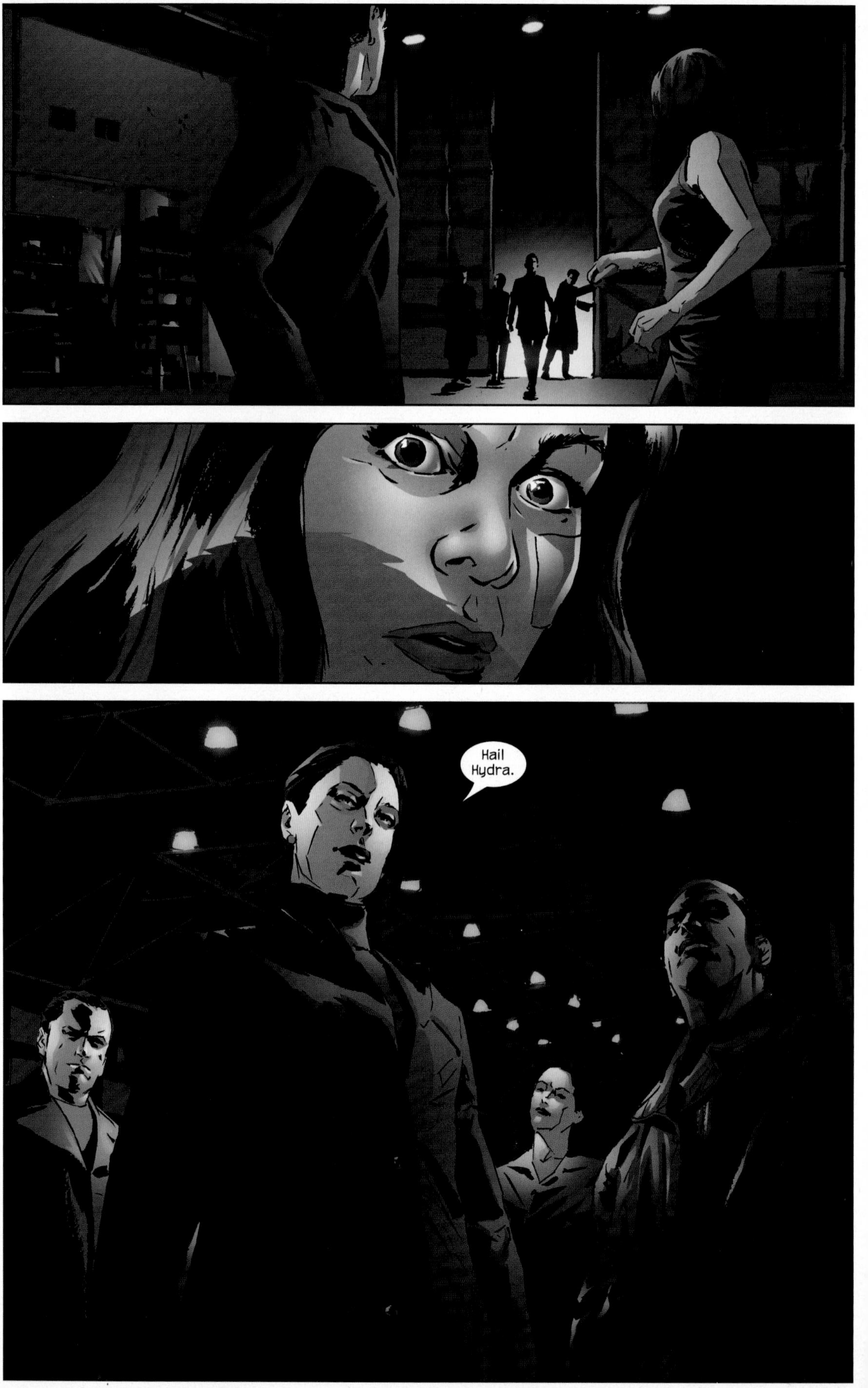
Hail Hydra.

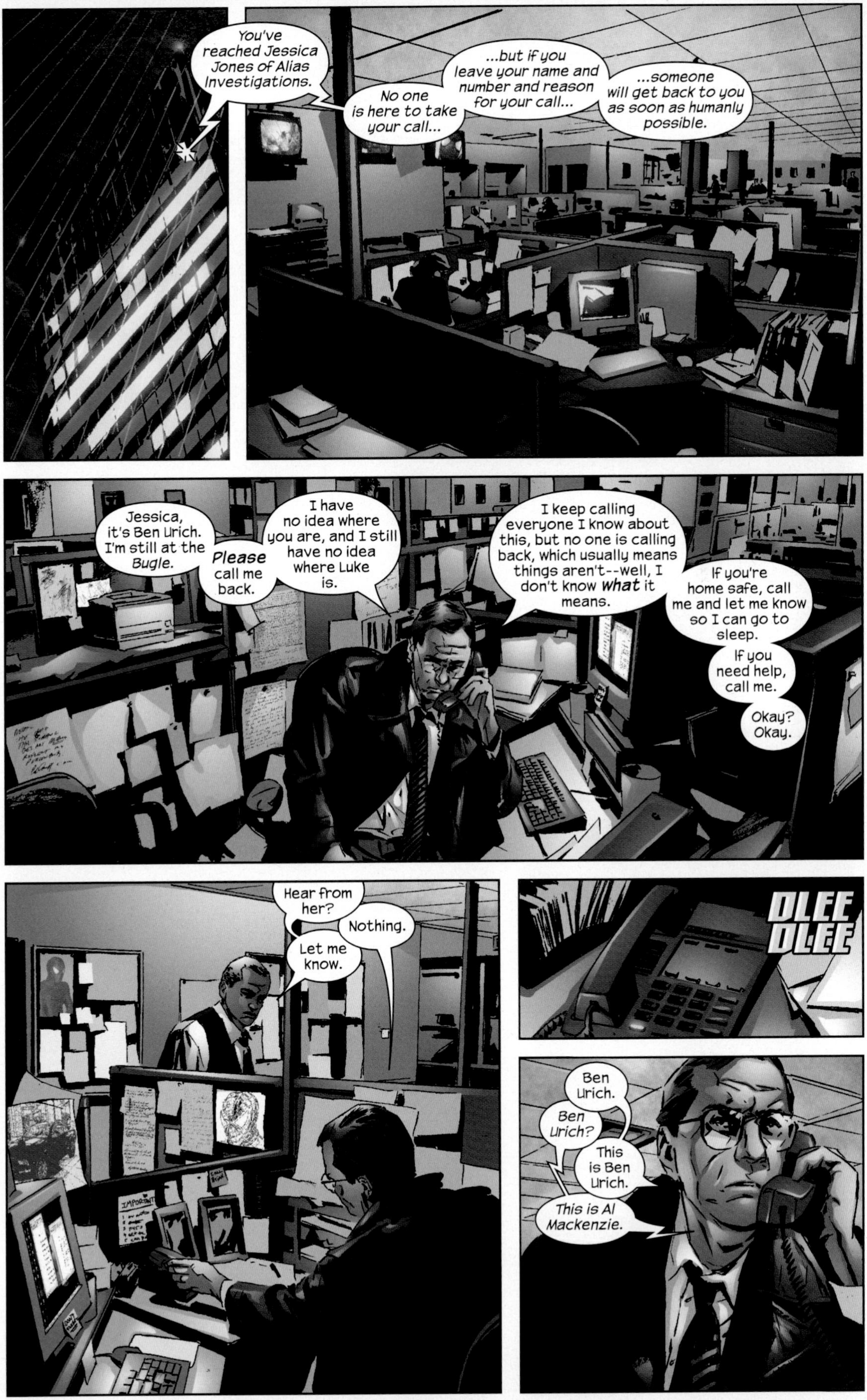
You've reached Jessica Jones of Alias Investigations.
No one is here to take your call...
...but if you leave your name and number and reason for your call...
...someone will get back to you as soon as humanly possible.
Jessica, it's Ben Urich. I'm still at the *Bugle.*
Please call me back.
I have no idea where you are, and I still have no idea where Luke is.
I keep calling everyone I know about this, but no one is calling back, which usually means things aren't--well, I don't know *what* it means.
If you're home safe, call me and let me know so I can go to sleep.
If you need help, call me.
Okay? Okay.
Hear from her?
Nothing.
Let me know.
DLEE DLEE
Ben Urich.
Ben Urich?
This is Ben Urich.
This is Al Mackenzie.

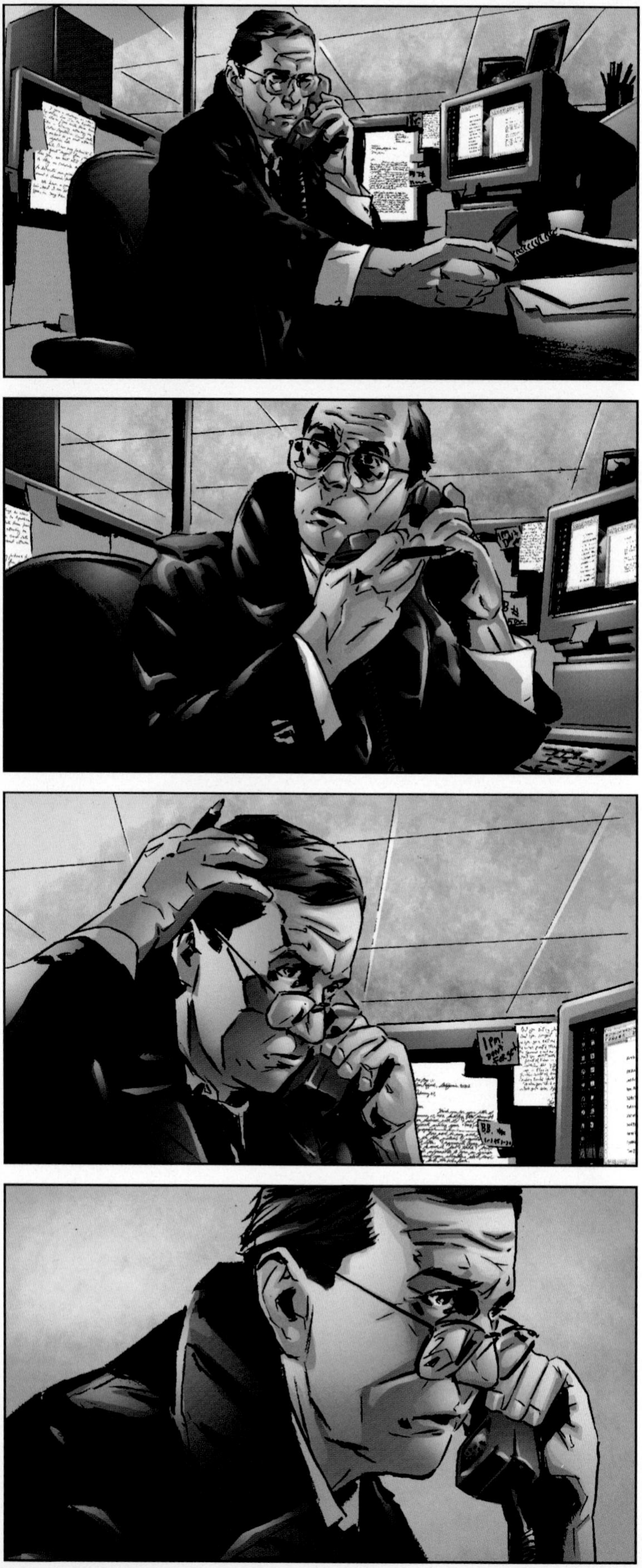

Ben: I'm sorry, I don't--

Al: Hmm, don't know how best to put this...

Al: ...but you helped me out a while back with something our friend...

Al: ...with the eye patch...

Ben: Ni--

Al: Don't! Don't say his name. If you say his name, it triggers a digital tap at the S.H.I.E.L.D. mainframe.

Ben: We're being bugged?

Al: No. No, don't be silly. You're being **monitored.** *You* **are** *a major media outlet.*

Ben: Monitored?

Al: Listen, I never thanked you for that thing you did for me that time.

Ben: Um. It wasn't me. It was my publisher.

Al: Don't be modest. I know it was you that went to him.

Ben: What can I do for you, Agent Mackenzie?

Al: What have you heard about something going down around your neck of the woods?

Ben: In New York?

Al: Yeah.

Ben: It's a big place.

Al: In some ways.

Ben: Like what?

Al: You'd know if you heard about it.

Ben: There's something that went on at a hospital.

Al: **That's** *the one.*

Ben: What happened?

Al: What did you hear?

Ben: Something that involved a guy we both know.

Al: With an eye patch.

Ben: Yes.

Al: Yeah.

Ben: Anything you want to tell me about it?

Al: Let's just say the patch $%#@ed up really bad.

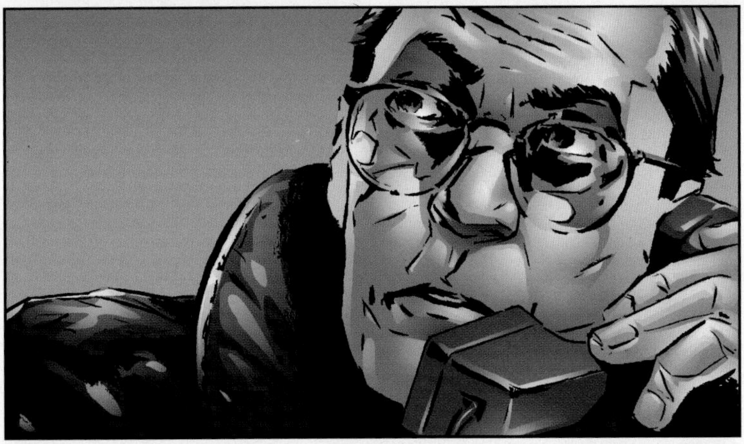

Ben: How?

Al: He did something he wasn't supposed to do and it came back to bite him on the ass.

Ben: What did he do?

Al: Something bad.

Ben: Something illegal?

Al: Even for him.

Ben: Really?

Al: If you wanted to report it, I'd say, go ahead.

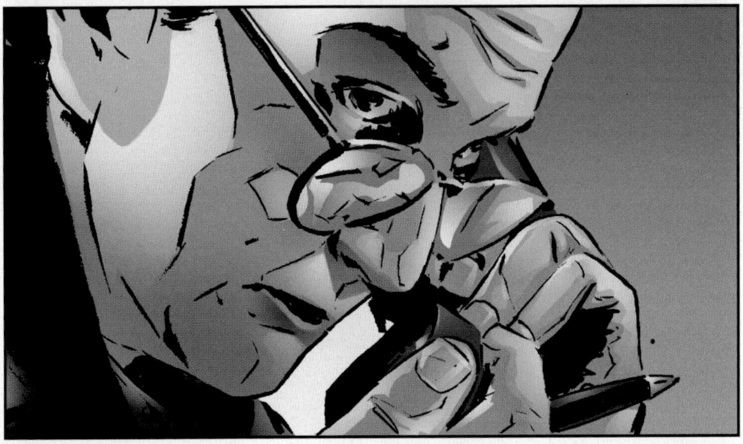

Ben: Report what?

Al: What happened.

Ben: We don't ***know*** what happened.

Al: You know that a major city hospital was attacked by a big load of tech-themed terrorists in retaliation for something someone did without the permission of the United States government or the United Nations.

Ben: Nick Fu--he--are you saying he attacked someone he wasn't supposed to and they attacked back? On American soil?

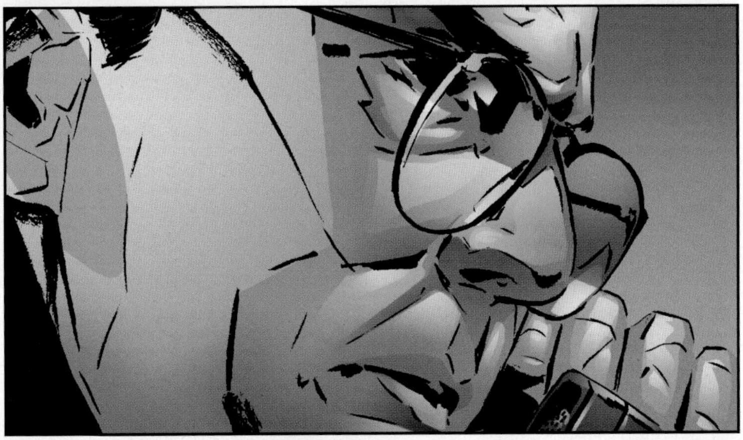

Al: You know that a lot of super heroes around the city were targeted for execution.

Ben: Is ***that*** what happened to Luke Cage?

*Al: See, you **do** have a story.*

Ben: Why is it ***okay*** to print this? Usually they put a blanket on us in the name of national security.

Al: I'm going to have to go now and call you maybe another time. We can get some lunch or something.

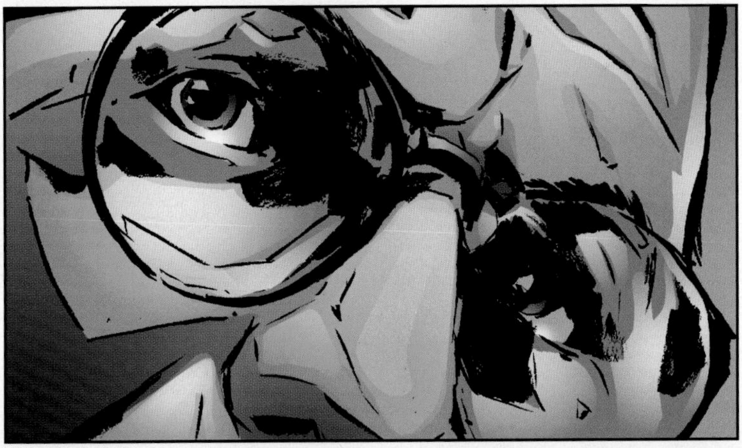

Ben: Answer me. Why is it okay to print this? Won't he--

Al: I wouldn't worry about the patch.

Ben: Did something happen to him?

Al: Not yet. But he's not going to be in a position to do anything to you if you do print this. Clearly, I can only be quoted as "an inside source."

Ben: Then tell me who attacked the hospital?

Al: You're not hearing me. It isn't "who", babe, it's "why"?

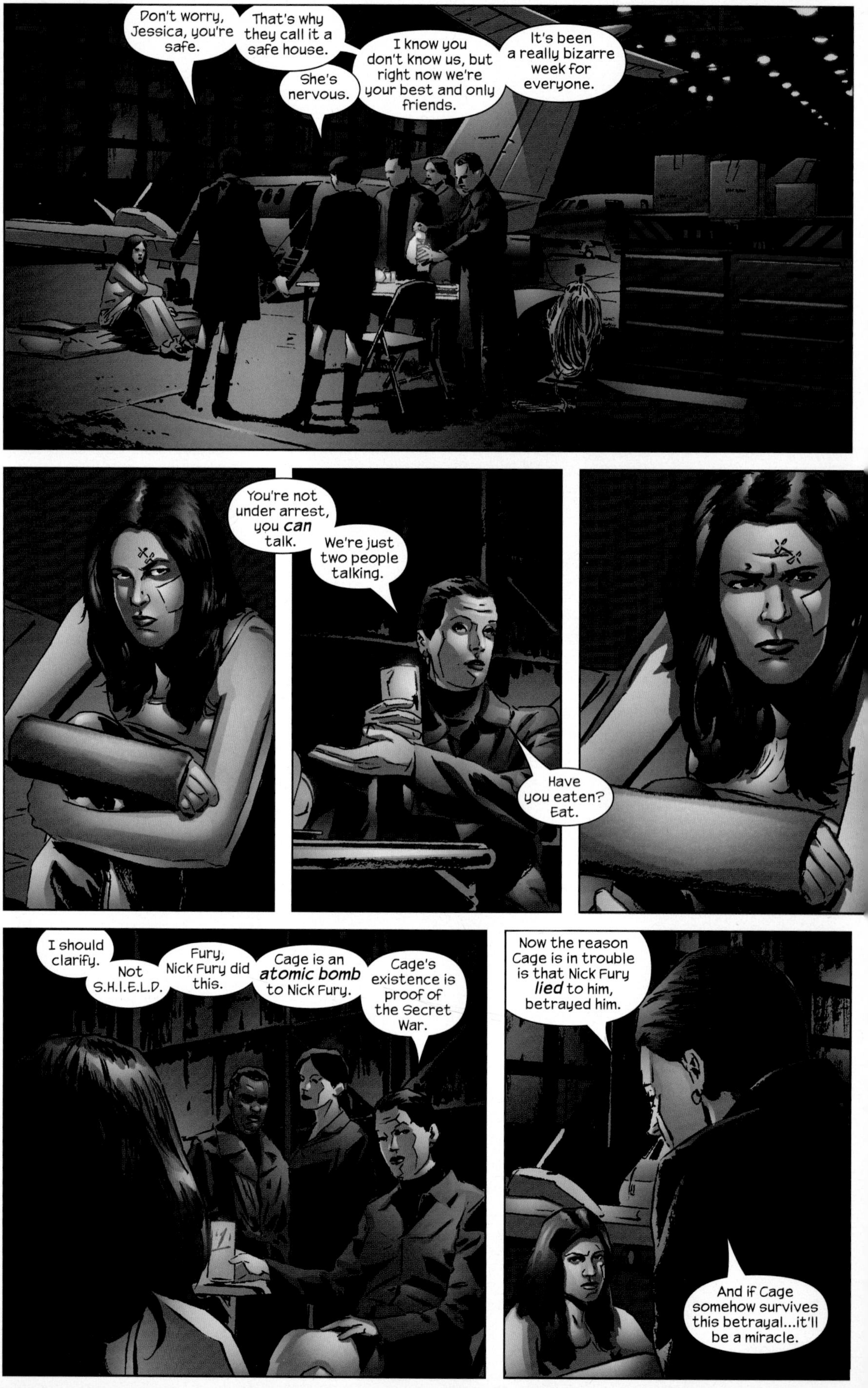

Don't worry, Jessica, you're safe.
That's why they call it a safe house.
She's nervous.
I know you don't know us, but right now we're your best and only friends.
It's been a really bizarre week for everyone.
You're not under arrest, you *can* talk.
We're just two people talking.
Have you eaten? Eat.
I should clarify.
Not S.H.I.E.L.D.
Fury, Nick Fury did this.
Cage is an *atomic bomb* to Nick Fury.
Cage's existence is proof of the Secret War.
Now the reason Cage is in trouble is that Nick Fury *lied* to him, betrayed him.
And if Cage somehow survives this betrayal...it'll be a miracle.

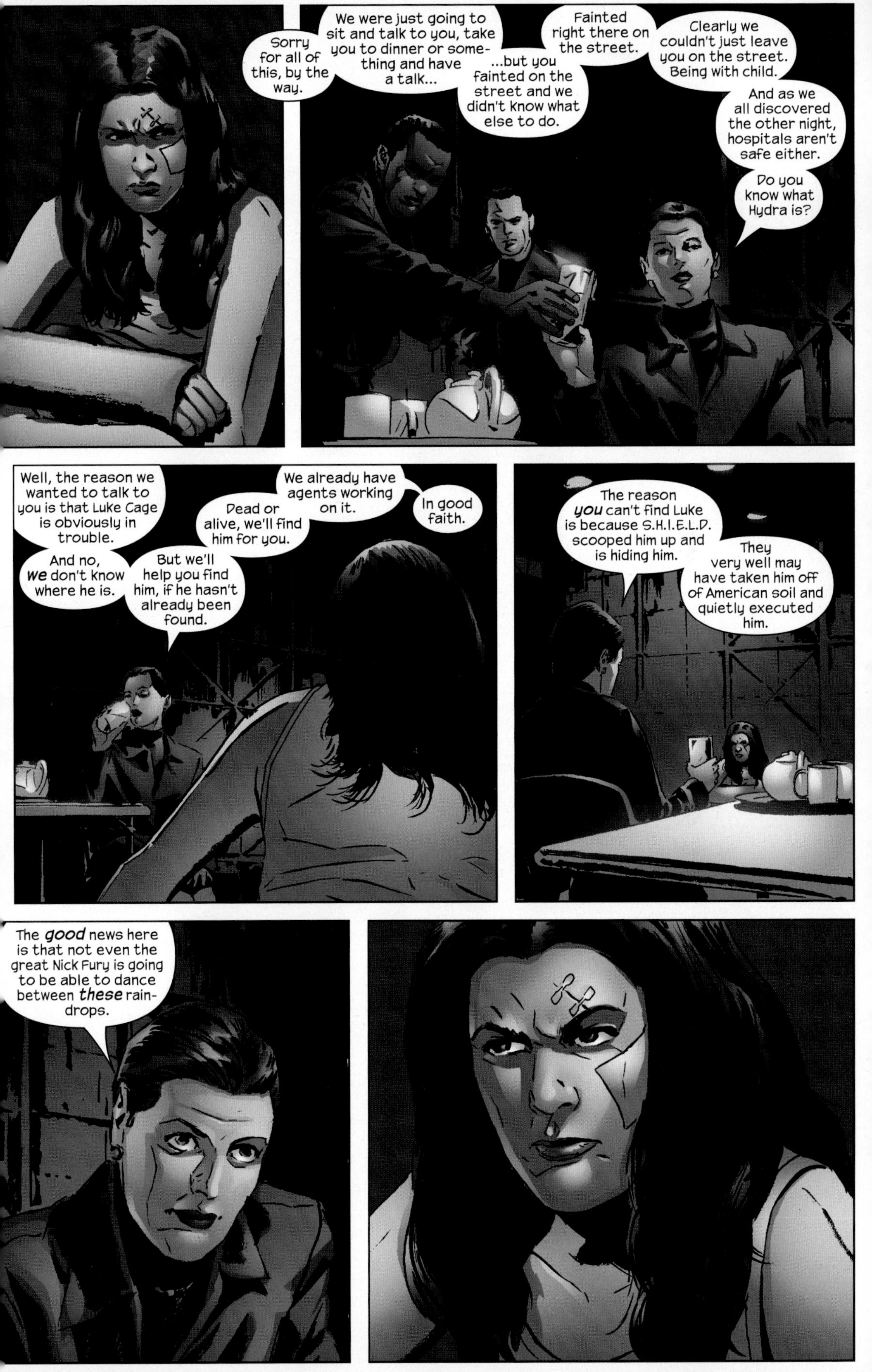

Sorry for all of this, by the way.
We were just going to sit and talk to you, take you to dinner or something and have a talk...
...but you fainted on the street and we didn't know what else to do.
Fainted right there on the street.
Clearly we couldn't just leave you on the street. Being with child.
And as we all discovered the other night, hospitals aren't safe either.
Do you know what Hydra is?
Well, the reason we wanted to talk to you is that Luke Cage is obviously in trouble.
And no, *we* don't know where he is.
But we'll help you find him, if he hasn't already been found.
Dead or alive, we'll find him for you.
We already have agents working on it.
In good faith.
The reason *you* can't find Luke is because S.H.I.E.L.D. scooped him up and is hiding him.
They very well may have taken him off of American soil and quietly executed him.
The *good* news here is that not even the great Nick Fury is going to be able to dance between *these* raindrops.

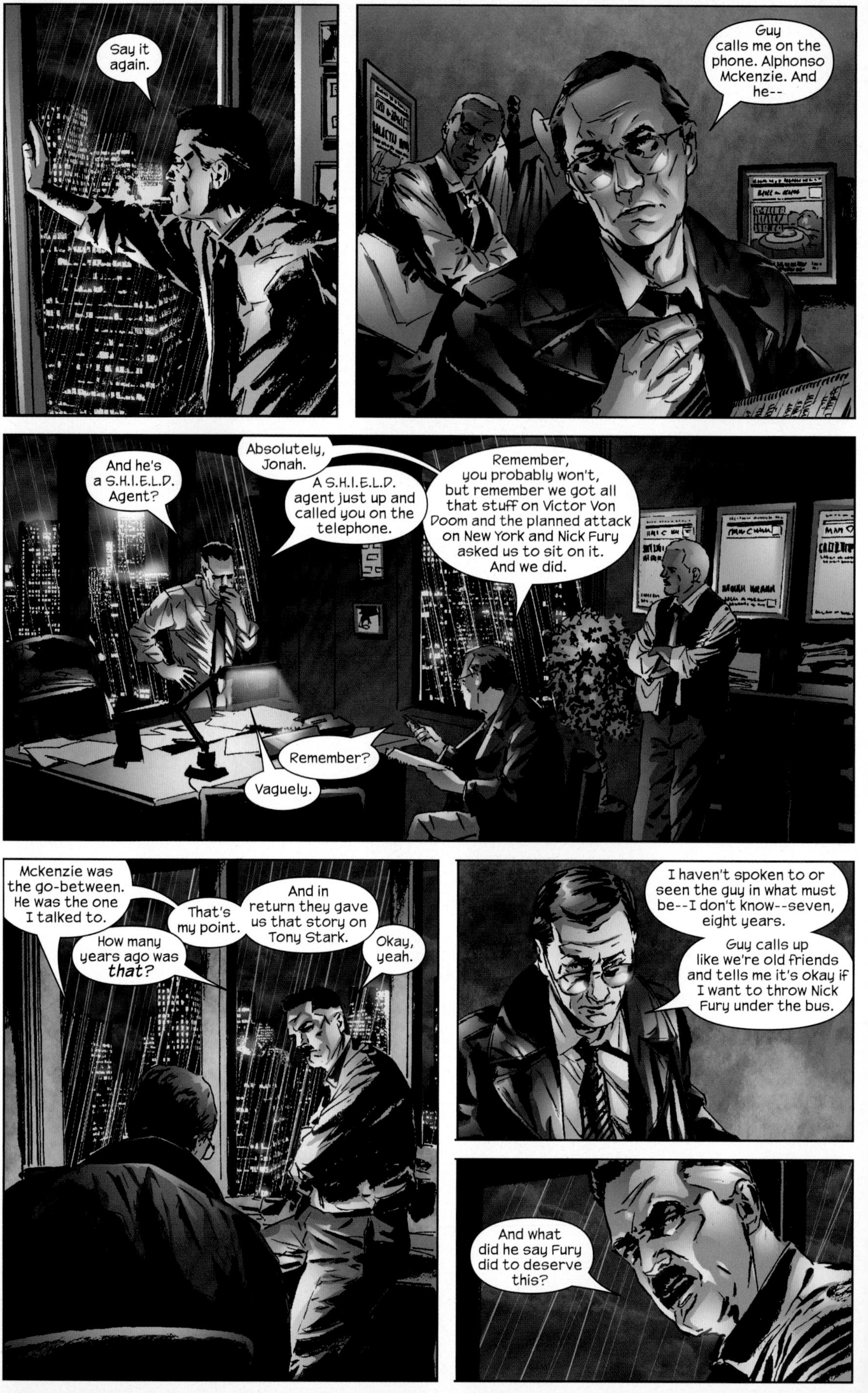
Say it again.
Guy calls me on the phone. Alphonso Mckenzie. And he--
And he's a S.H.I.E.L.D. Agent?
Absolutely, Jonah.
A S.H.I.E.L.D. agent just up and called you on the telephone.
Remember, you probably won't, but remember we got all that stuff on Victor Von Doom and the planned attack on New York and Nick Fury asked us to sit on it. And we did.
Remember?
Vaguely.
Mckenzie was the go-between. He was the one I talked to.
How many years ago was *that*?
That's my point.
And in return they gave us that story on Tony Stark.
Okay, yeah.
I haven't spoken to or seen the guy in what must be--I don't know--seven, eight years.
Guy calls up like we're old friends and tells me it's okay if I want to throw Nick Fury under the bus.
And what did he say Fury did to deserve this?

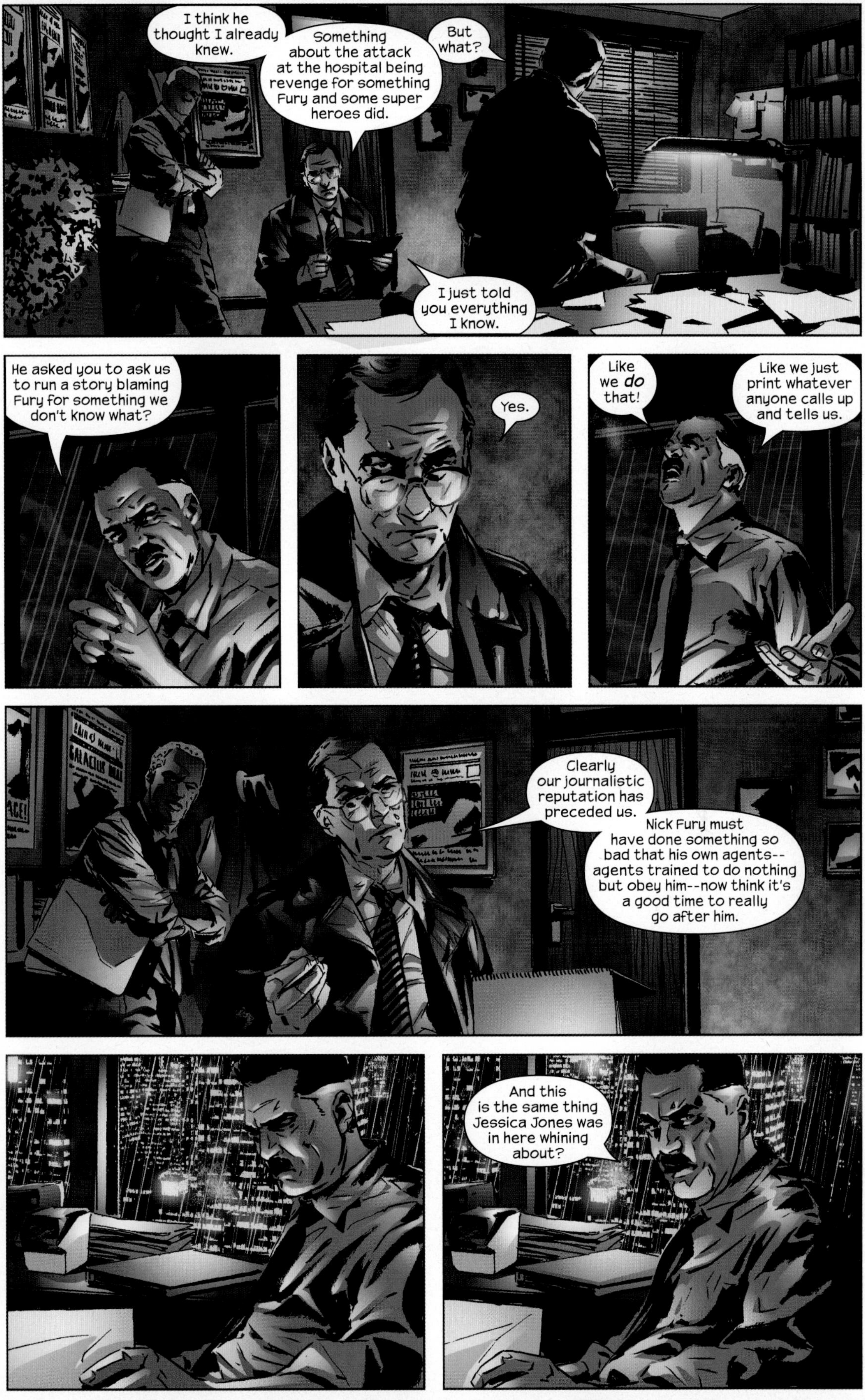
I think he thought I already knew.
Something about the attack at the hospital being revenge for something Fury and some super heroes did.
But what?
I just told you everything I know.
He asked you to ask us to run a story blaming Fury for something we don't know what?
Yes.
Like we *do* that!
Like we just print whatever anyone calls up and tells us.
Clearly our journalistic reputation has preceded us.
Nick Fury must have done something so bad that his own agents--agents trained to do nothing but obey him--now think it's a good time to really go after him.
And this is the same thing Jessica Jones was in here whining about?

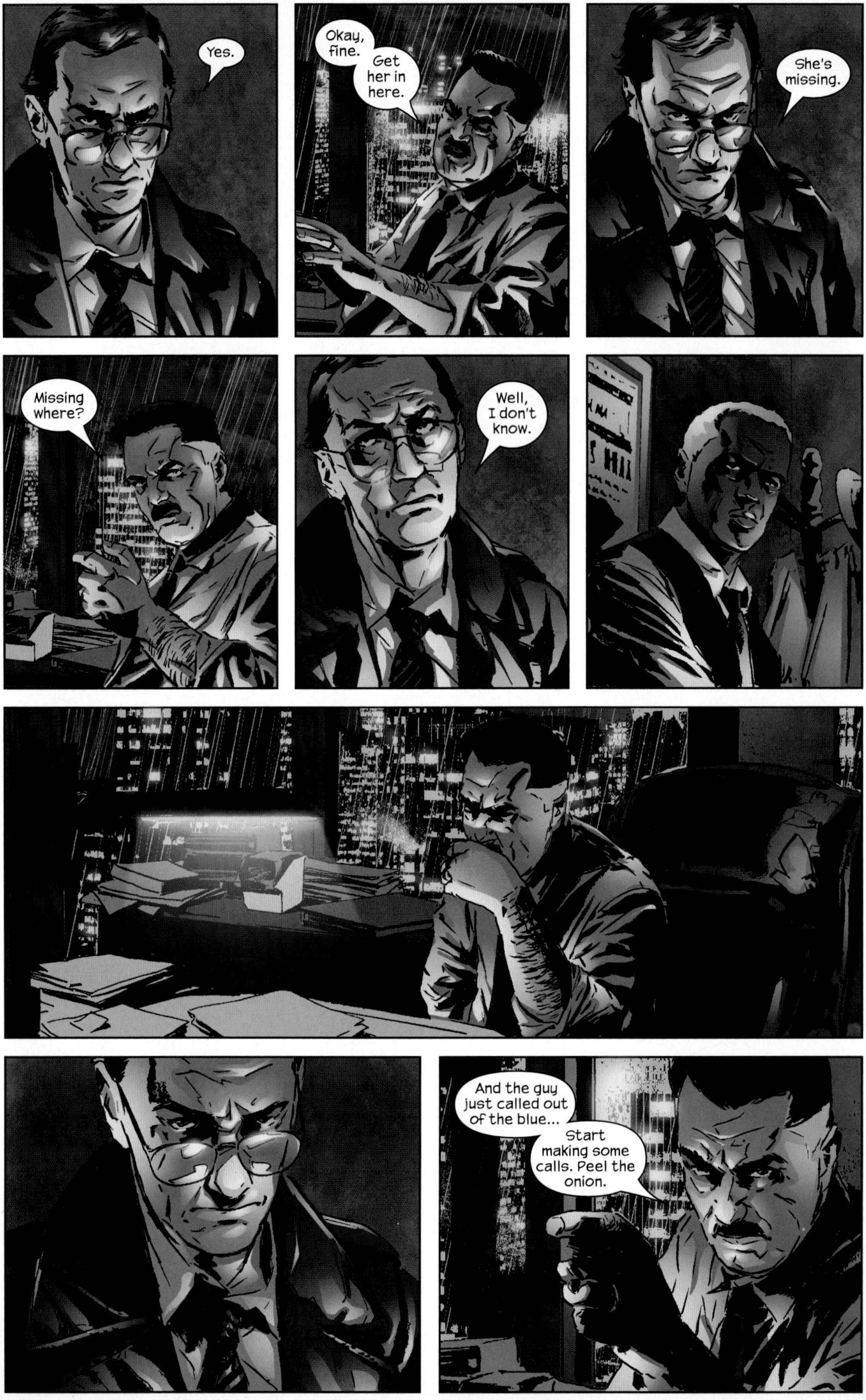
Yes.
Okay, fine.
Get her in here.
She's missing.
Missing where?
Well, I don't know.
And the guy just called out of the blue...
Start making some calls. Peel the onion.

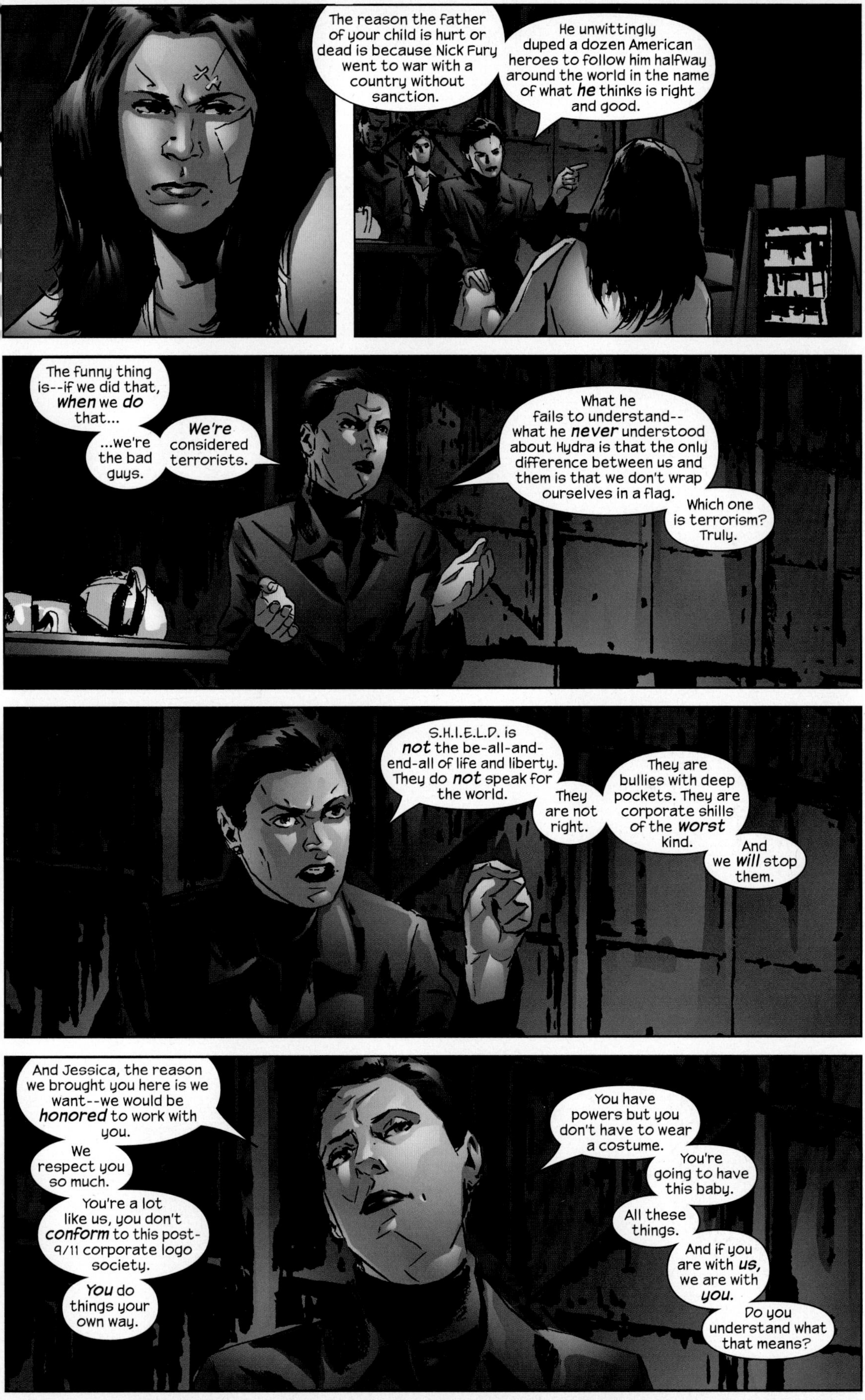
The reason the father of your child is hurt or dead is because Nick Fury went to war with a country without sanction.
He unwittingly duped a dozen American heroes to follow him halfway around the world in the name of what *he* thinks is right and good.
The funny thing is--if we did that, *when* we *do* that...
...we're the bad guys.
We're considered terrorists.
What he fails to understand--what he *never* understood about Hydra is that the only difference between us and them is that we don't wrap ourselves in a flag.
Which one is terrorism? Truly.
S.H.I.E.L.D. is *not* the be-all-and-end-all of life and liberty. They do *not* speak for the world.
They are not right.
They are bullies with deep pockets. They are corporate shills of the *worst* kind.
And we *will* stop them.
And Jessica, the reason we brought you here is we want--we would be *honored* to work with you.
We respect you so much.
You're a lot like us, you don't *conform* to this post-9/11 corporate logo society.
You do things your own way.
You have powers but you don't have to wear a costume.
You're going to have this baby.
All these things.
And if you are with *us*, we are with *you*.
Do you understand what that means?

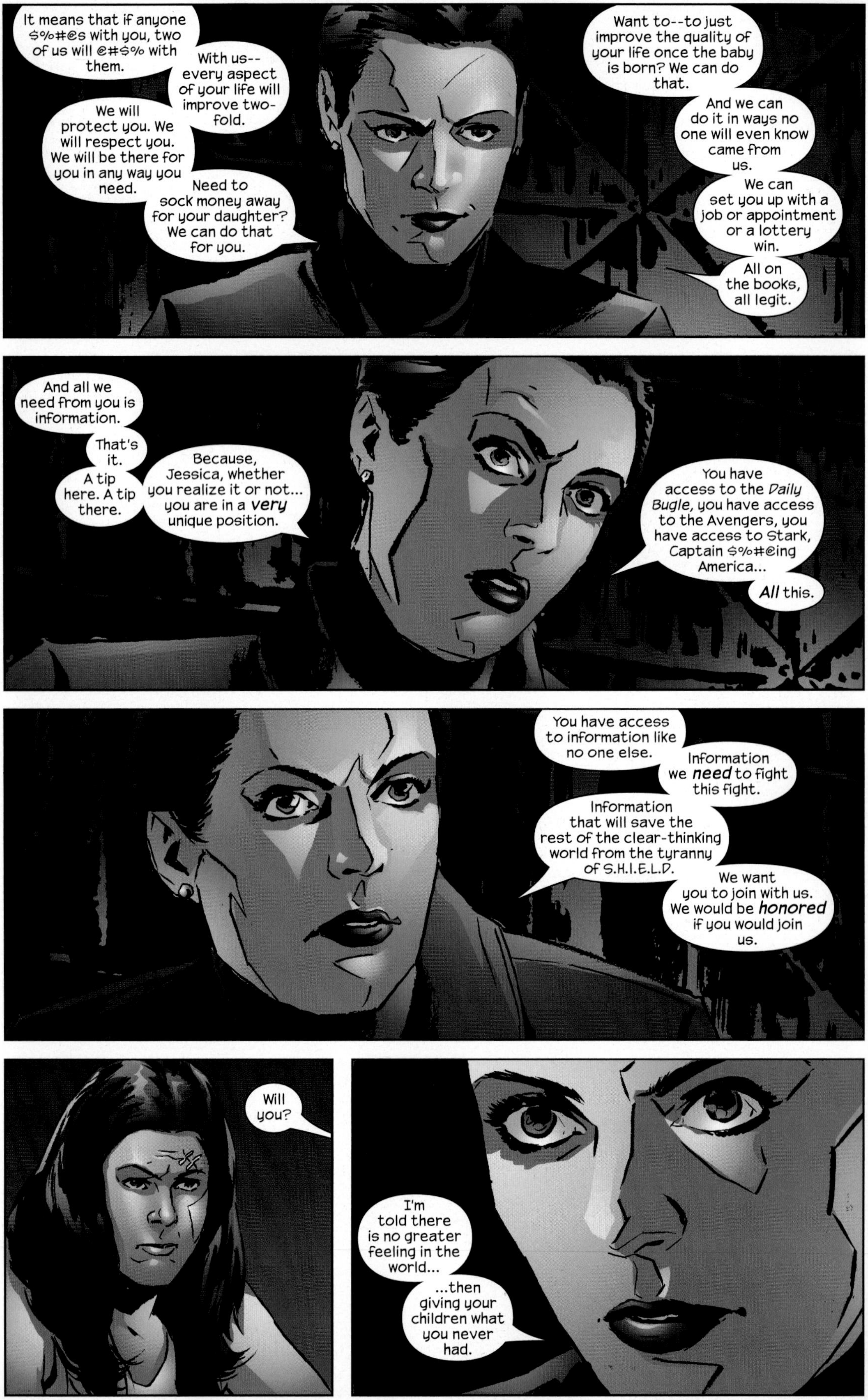

It means that if anyone $%#@s with you, two of us will @#$% with them.
With us--every aspect of your life will improve two-fold.
We will protect you. We will respect you. We will be there for you in any way you need.
Need to sock money away for your daughter? We can do that for you.
Want to--to just improve the quality of your life once the baby is born? We can do that.
And we can do it in ways no one will even know came from us.
We can set you up with a job or appointment or a lottery win.
All on the books, all legit.
And all we need from you is information.
That's it.
A tip here. A tip there.
Because, Jessica, whether you realize it or not... you are in a *very* unique position.
You have access to the *Daily Bugle*, you have access to the Avengers, you have access to Stark, Captain $%#@ing America...
All this.
You have access to information like no one else.
Information we ***need*** to fight this fight.
Information that will save the rest of the clear-thinking world from the tyranny of S.H.I.E.L.D.
We want you to join with us. We would be ***honored*** if you would join us.
Will you?
I'm told there is no greater feeling in the world...
...then giving your children what you never had.

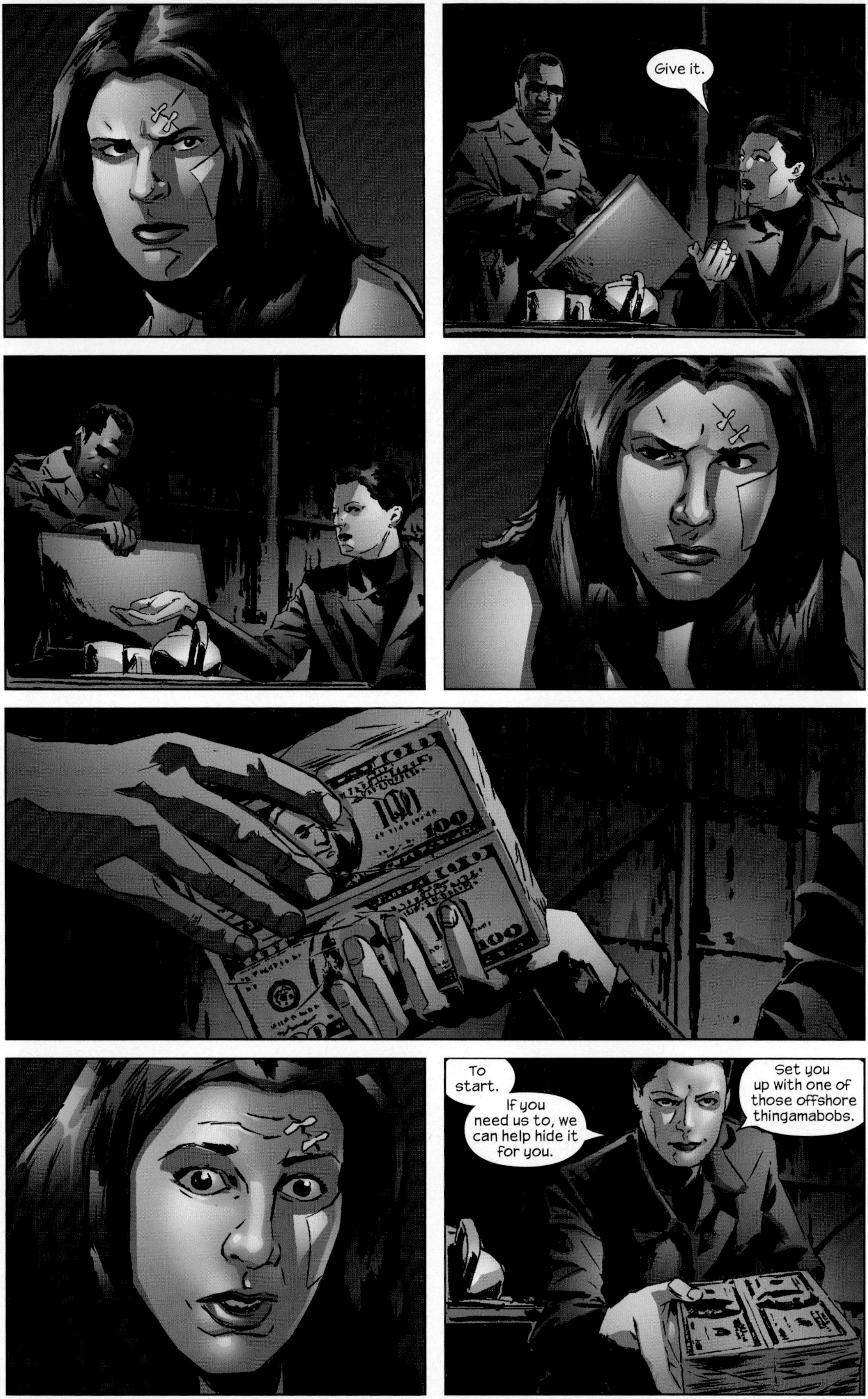
Give it.
To start.
If you need us to, we can help hide it for you.
Set you up with one of those offshore thingamabobs.

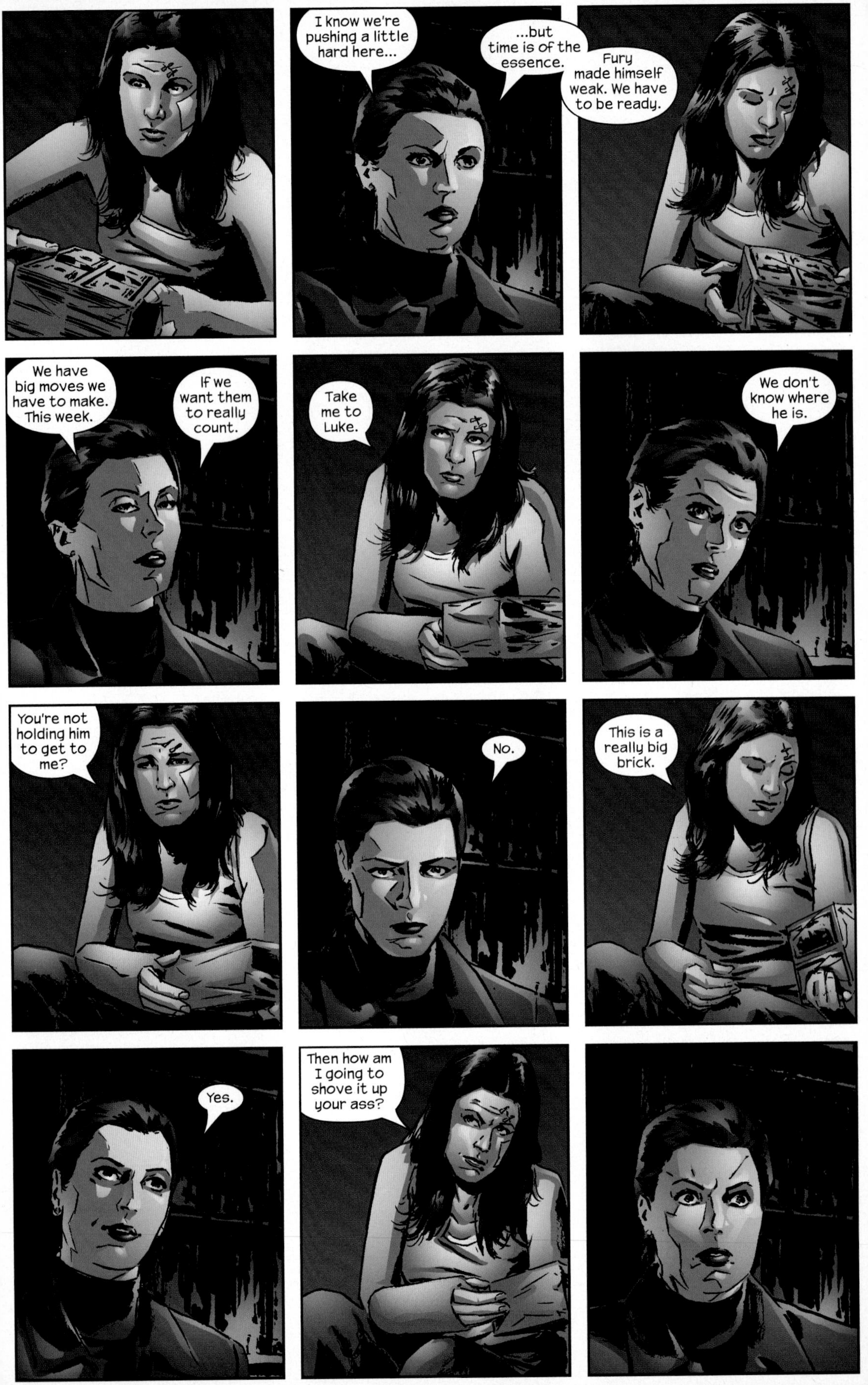
I know we're pushing a little hard here...
...but time is of the essence.
Fury made himself weak. We have to be ready.
We have big moves we have to make. This week.
If we want them to really count.
Take me to Luke.
We don't know where he is.
You're not holding him to get to me?
No.
This is a really big brick.
Yes.
Then how am I going to shove it up your ass?

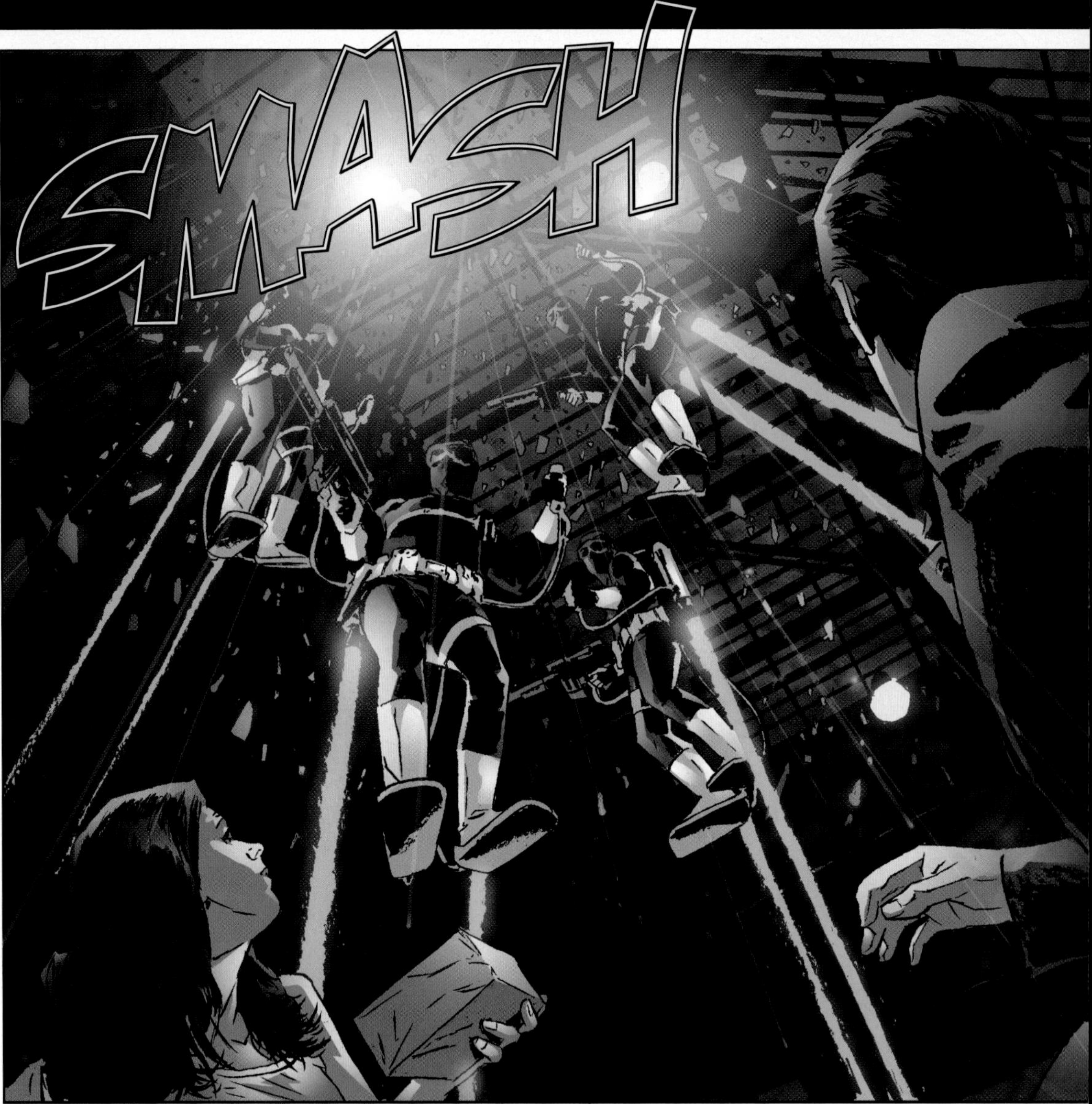
SMASH

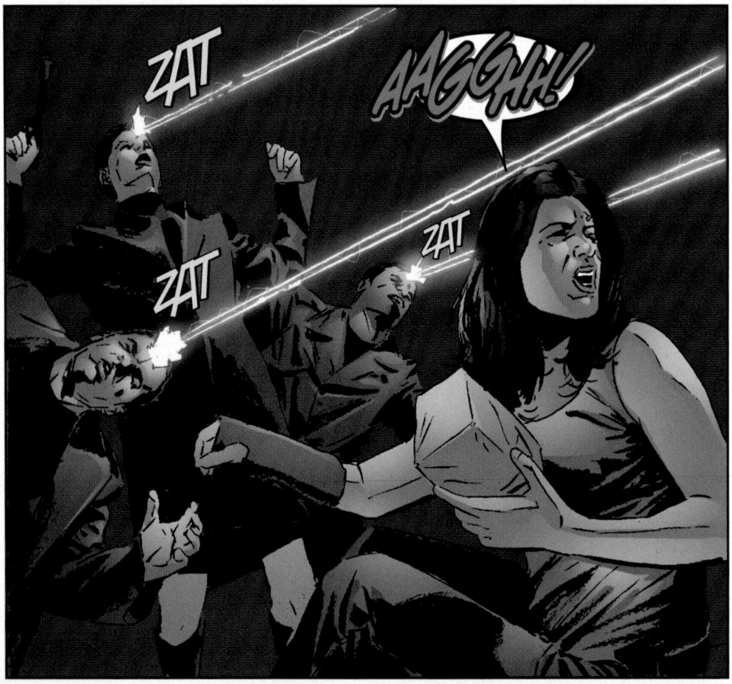
ZAT
AAGGHH!
ZAT
ZAT

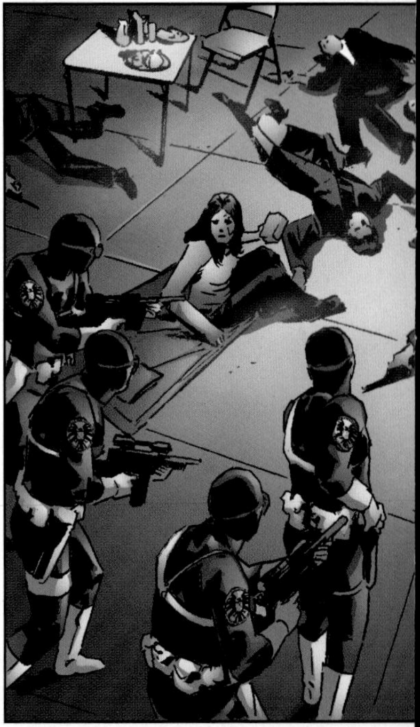

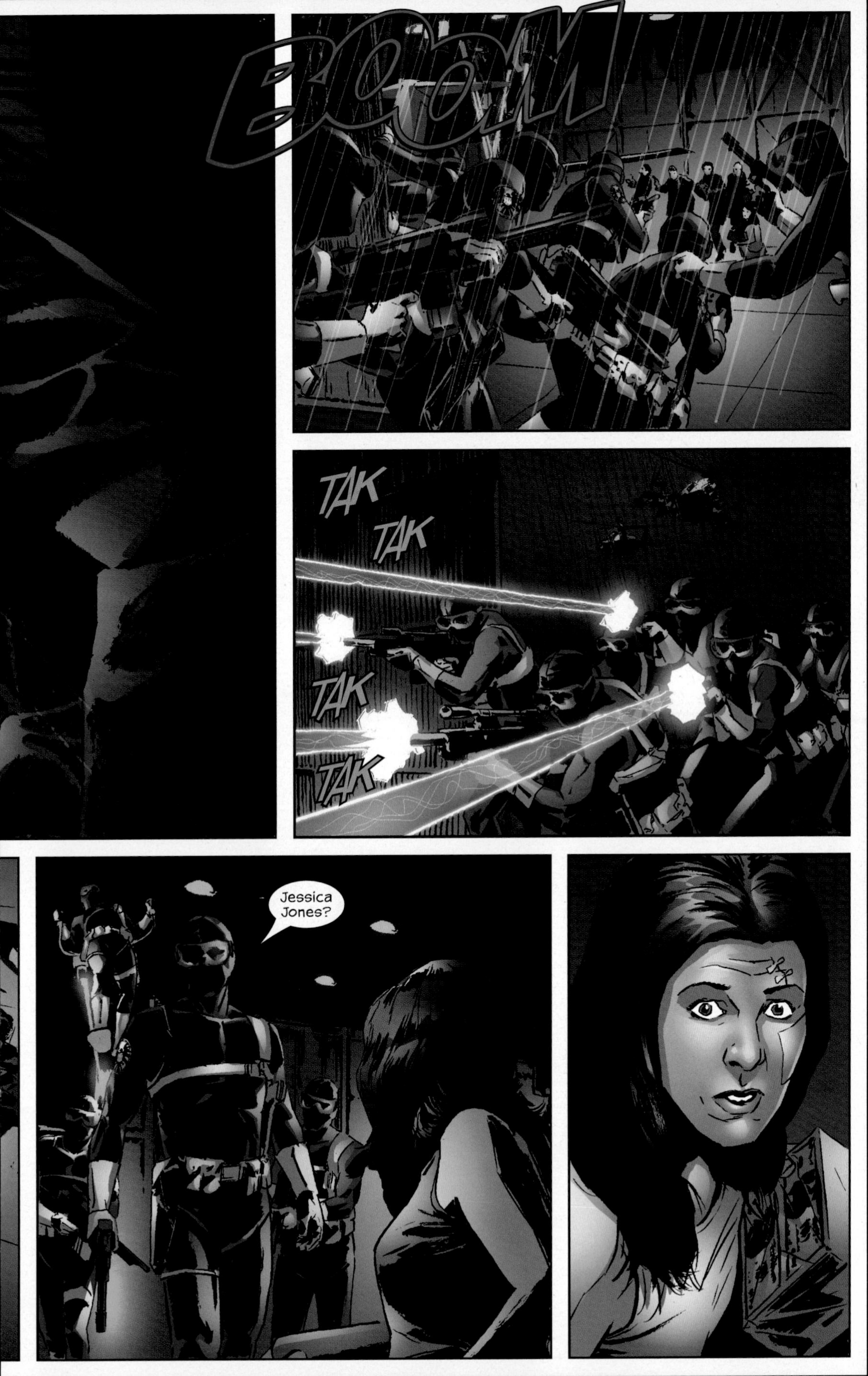
BOOM
TAK
TAK
TAK
TAK
Jessica Jones?

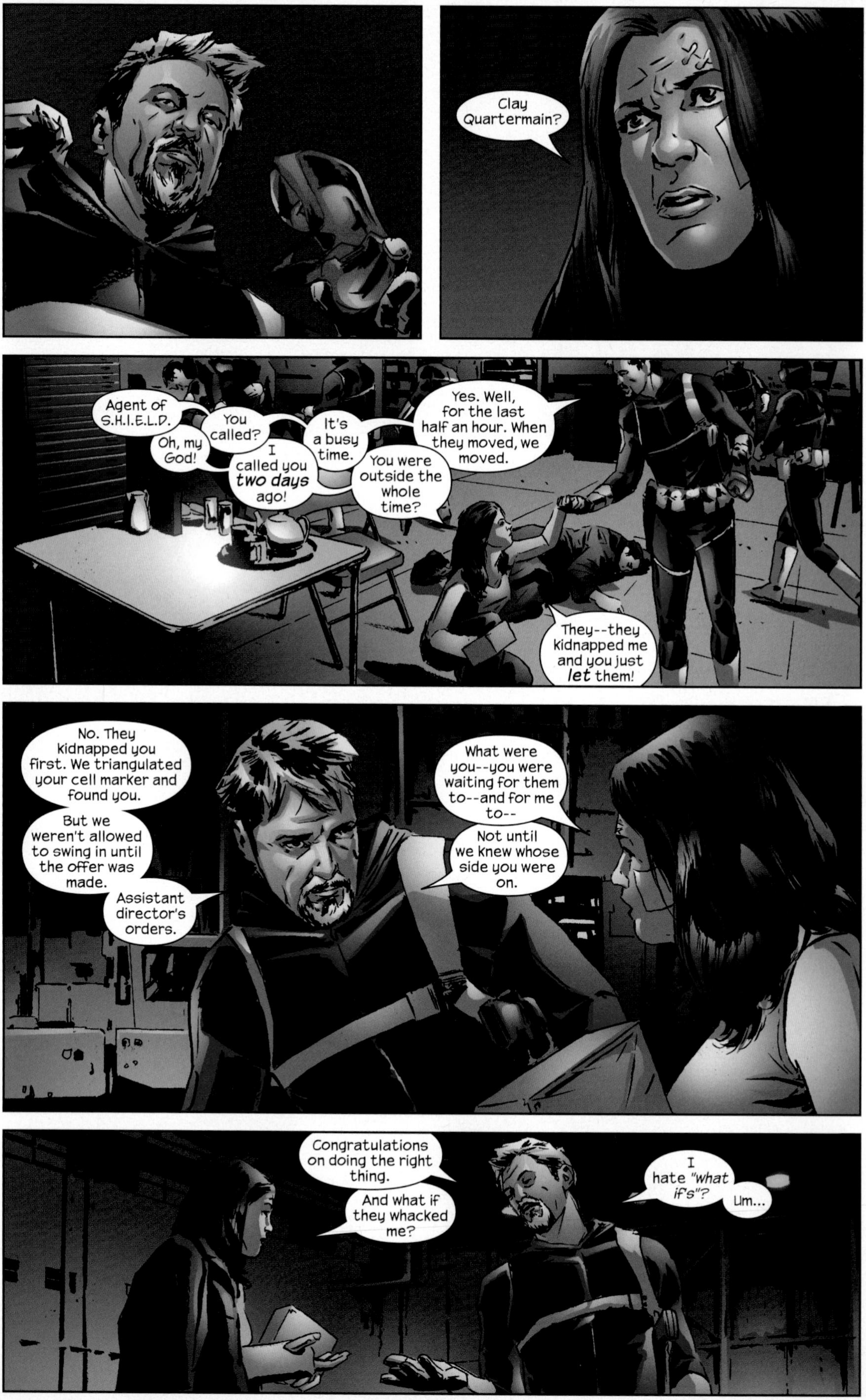
Clay Quartermain?
Agent of S.H.I.E.L.D.
You called?
Oh, my God!
I called you *two days* ago!
It's a busy time.
You were outside the whole time?
Yes. Well, for the last half an hour. When they moved, we moved.
They--they kidnapped me and you just *let* them!
No. They kidnapped you first. We triangulated your cell marker and found you.
But we weren't allowed to swing in until the offer was made.
Assistant director's orders.
What were you--you were waiting for them to--and for me to--
Not until we knew whose side you were on.
Congratulations on doing the right thing.
And what if they whacked me?
I hate *"what if's"*?
Um...

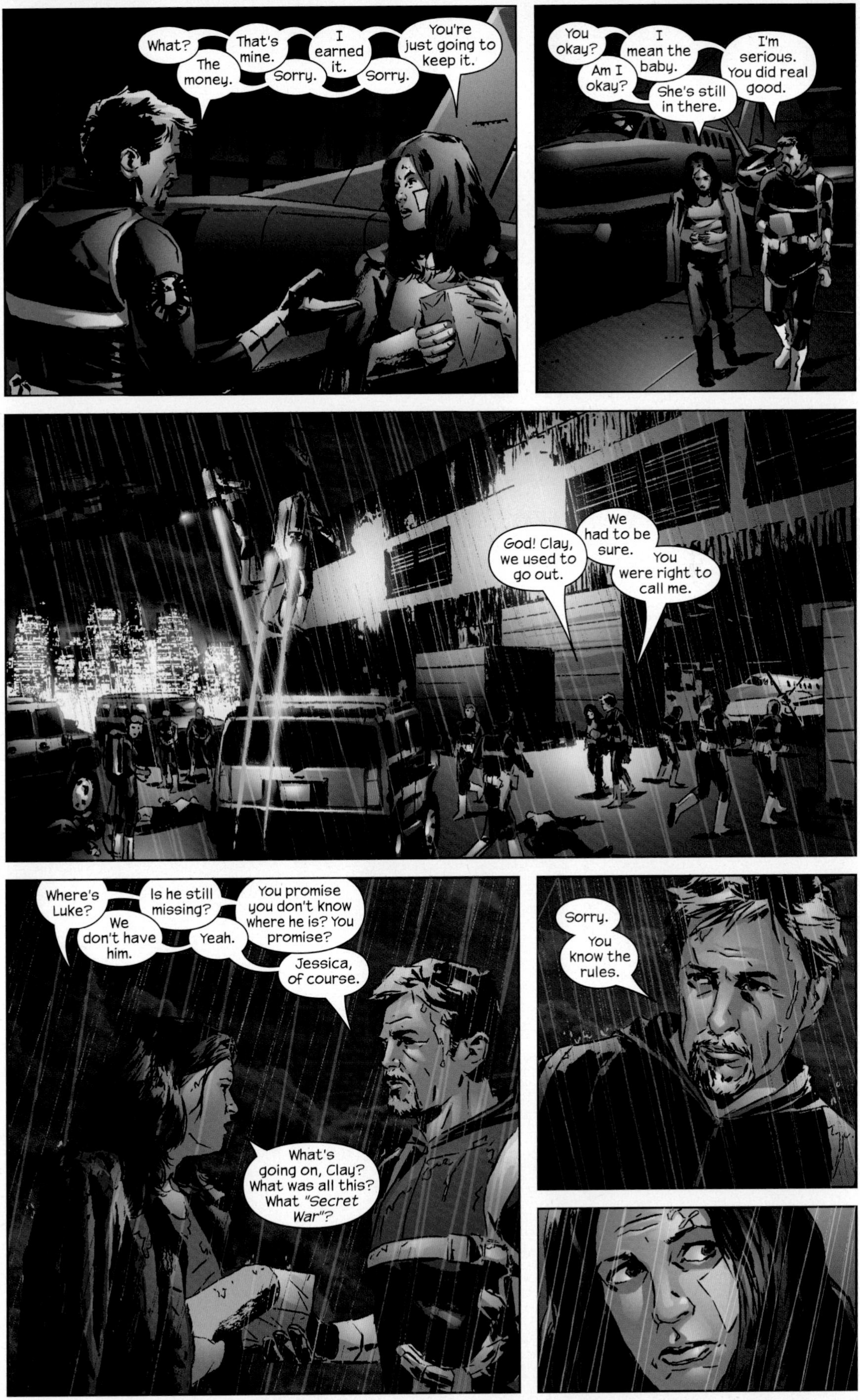

What?
The money.
That's mine.
Sorry.
I earned it.
Sorry.
You're just going to keep it.
You okay?
Am I okay?
I mean the baby.
She's still in there.
I'm serious. You did real good.
God! Clay, we used to go out.
We had to be sure.
You were right to call me.
Where's Luke?
We don't have him.
Is he still missing?
Yeah.
You promise you don't know where he is? You promise?
Jessica, of course.
What's going on, Clay? What was all this? What "Secret War"?
Sorry.
You know the rules.

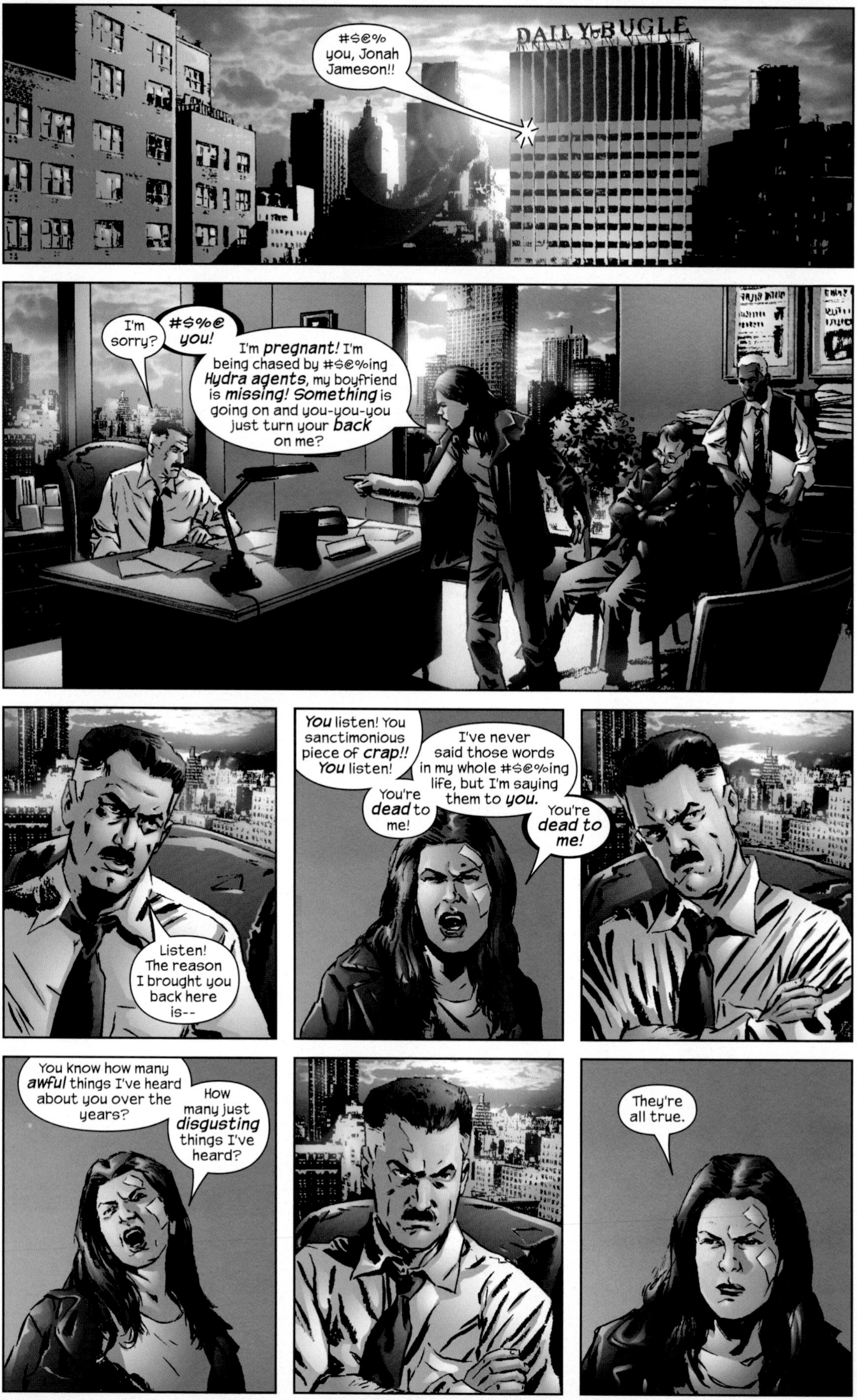
DAILY BUGLE
#$@% you, Jonah Jameson!!
I'm sorry?
#$%@ you!
I'm pregnant! I'm being chased by #$@%ing Hydra agents, my boyfriend is missing! Something is going on and you-you-you just turn your back on me?
Listen! The reason I brought you back here is--
You listen! You sanctimonious piece of crap!! You listen!
You're dead to me!
I've never said those words in my whole #$@%ing life, but I'm saying them to you.
You're dead to me!
You know how many awful things I've heard about you over the years?
How many just disgusting things I've heard?
They're all true.

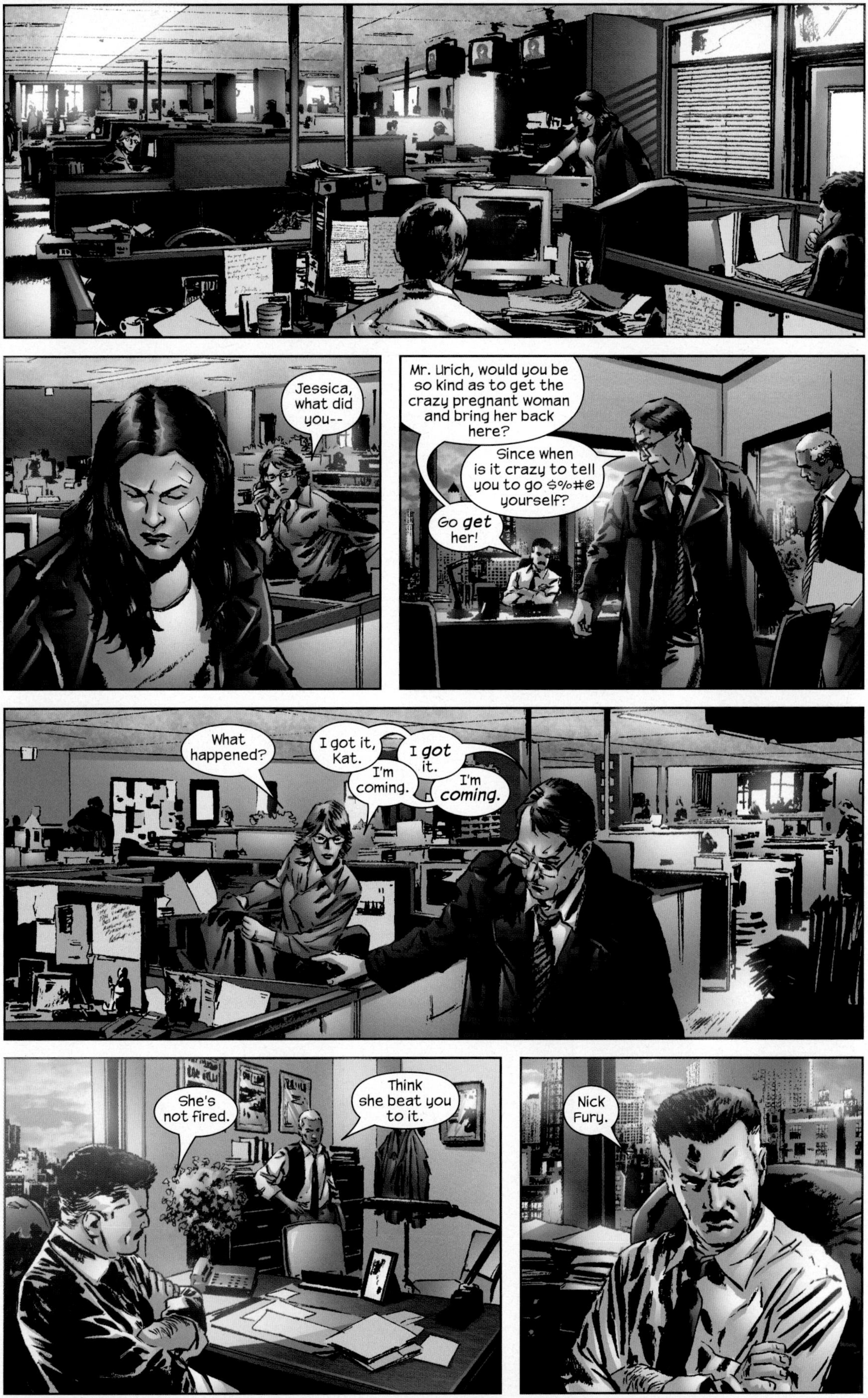

Jessica, what did you--
Mr. Urich, would you be so kind as to get the crazy pregnant woman and bring her back here?
Since when is it crazy to tell you to go $%#@ yourself?
Go get her!
What happened?
I got it, Kat.
I'm coming.
I got it.
I'm coming.
She's not fired.
Think she beat you to it.
Nick Fury.

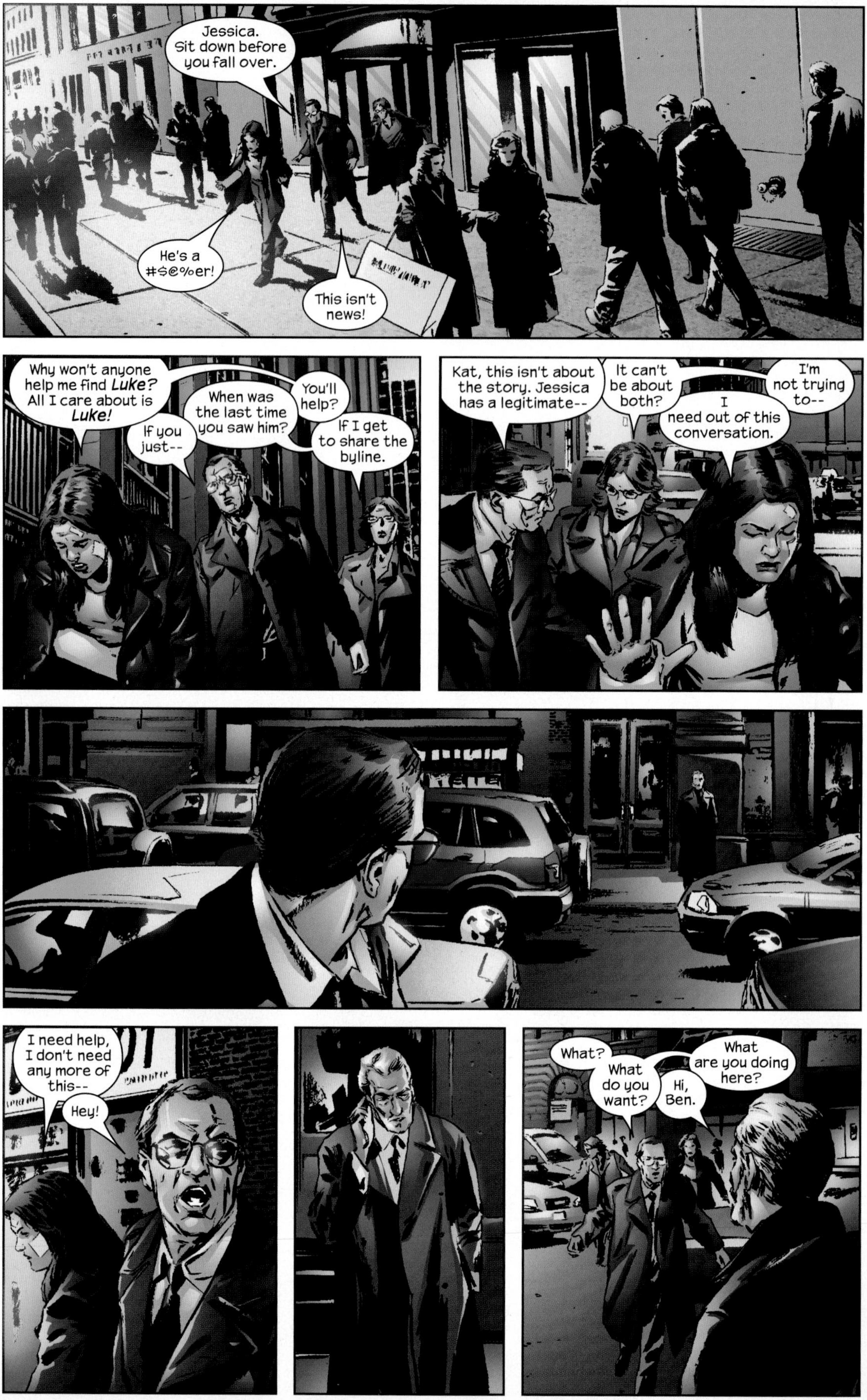
Jessica. Sit down before you fall over.
He's a #$@%er!
This isn't news!
Why won't anyone help me find *Luke?* All I care about is *Luke!*
If you just--
When was the last time you saw him?
You'll help?
If I get to share the byline.
Kat, this isn't about the story. Jessica has a legitimate--
It can't be about both?
I'm not trying to--
I need out of this conversation.
I need help, I don't need any more of this--
Hey!
What?
What do you want?
Hi, Ben.
What are you doing here?

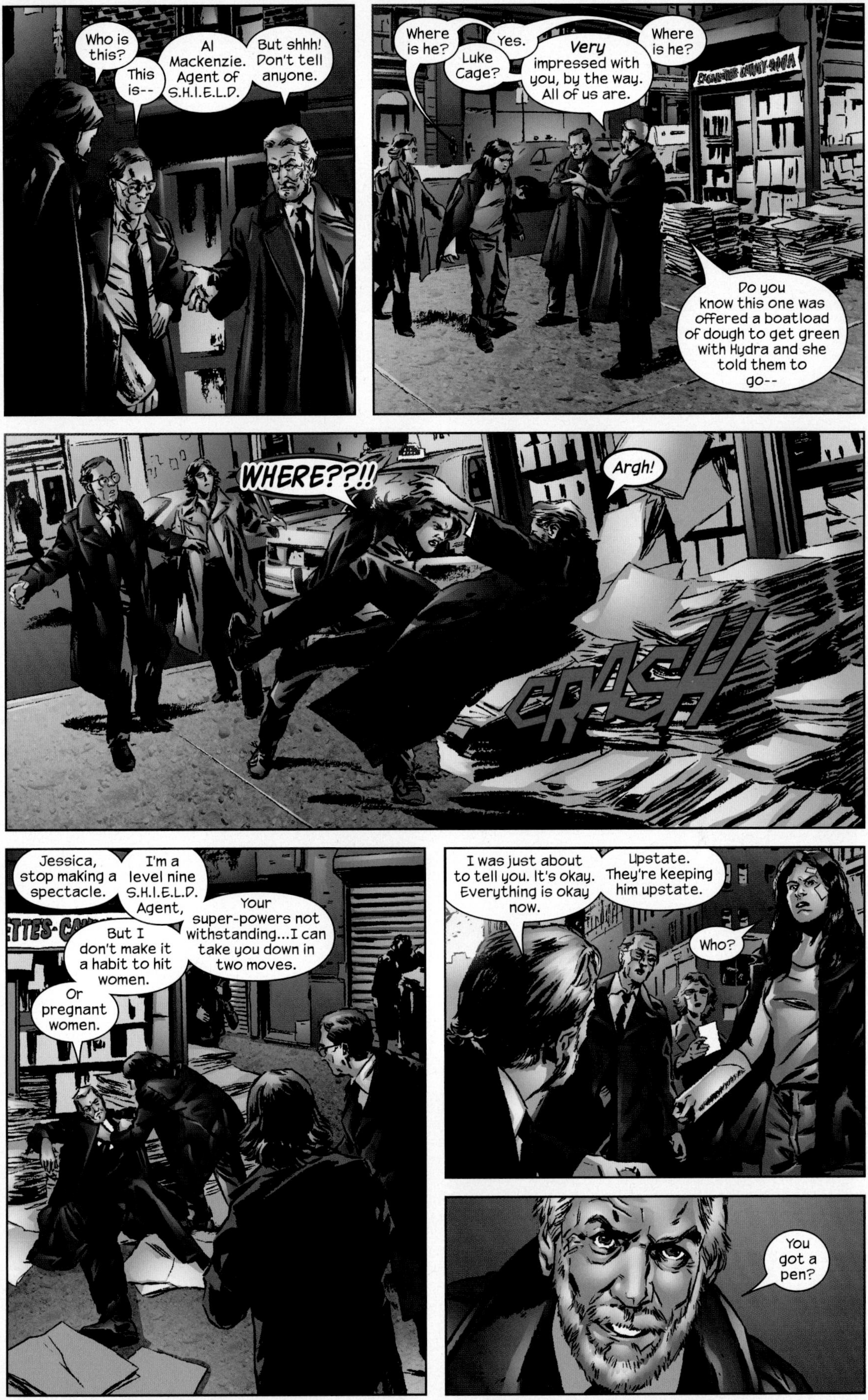
Who is this?
This is--
Al Mackenzie. Agent of S.H.I.E.L.D.
But shhh! Don't tell anyone.
Where is he?
Luke Cage?
Yes.
Very impressed with you, by the way. All of us are.
Where is he?
Do you know this one was offered a boatload of dough to get green with Hydra and she told them to go--
WHERE??!!
Argh!
CRASH
Jessica, stop making a spectacle.
I'm a level nine S.H.I.E.L.D. Agent,
But I don't make it a habit to hit women.
Or pregnant women.
Your super-powers not withstanding...I can take you down in two moves.
I was just about to tell you. It's okay. Everything is okay now.
Upstate. They're keeping him upstate.
Who?
You got a pen?

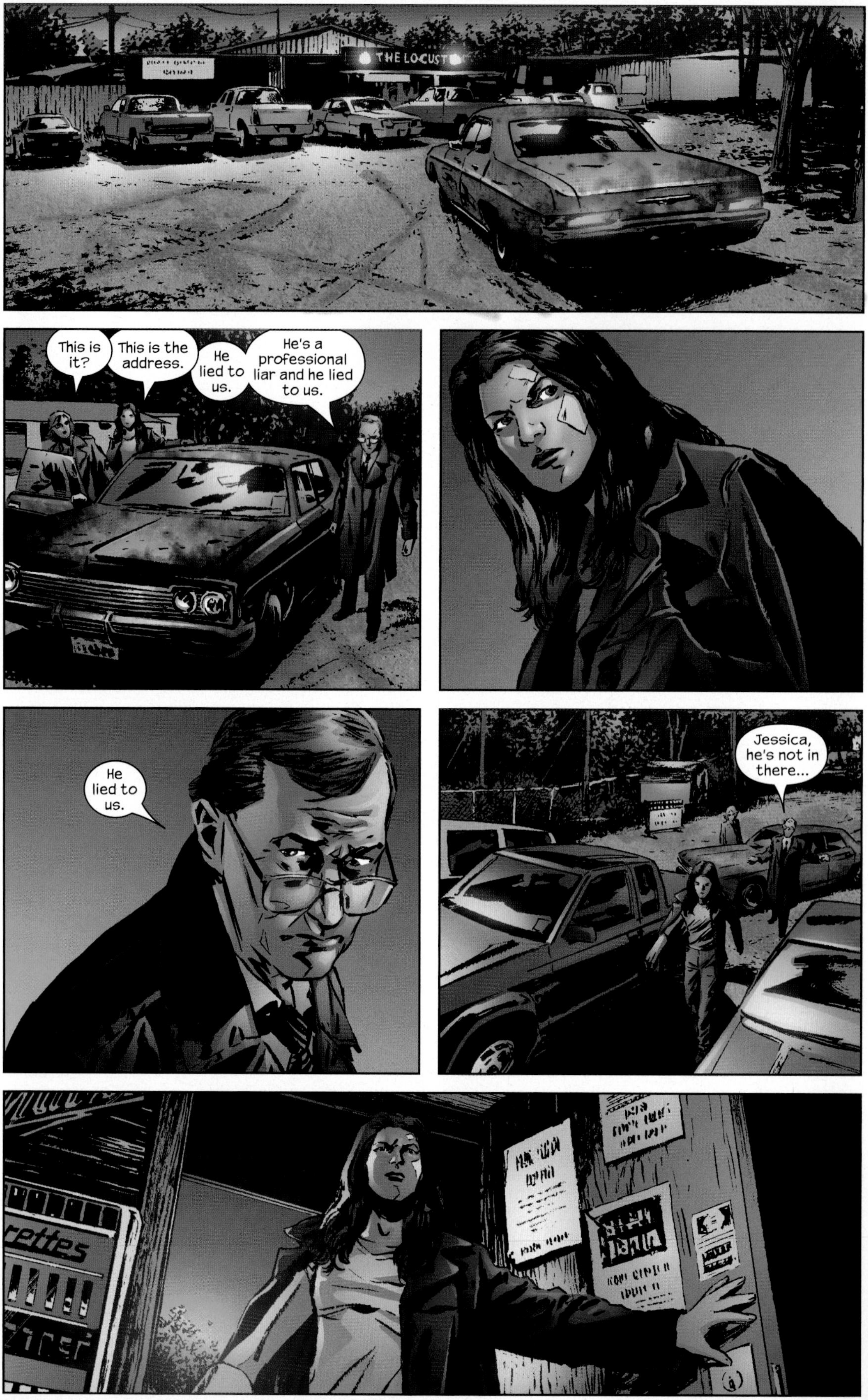
THE LOCUST
This is it?
This is the address.
He lied to us.
He's a professional liar and he lied to us.
He lied to us.
Jessica, he's not in there...

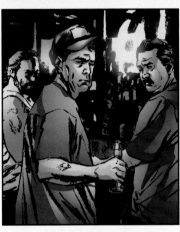

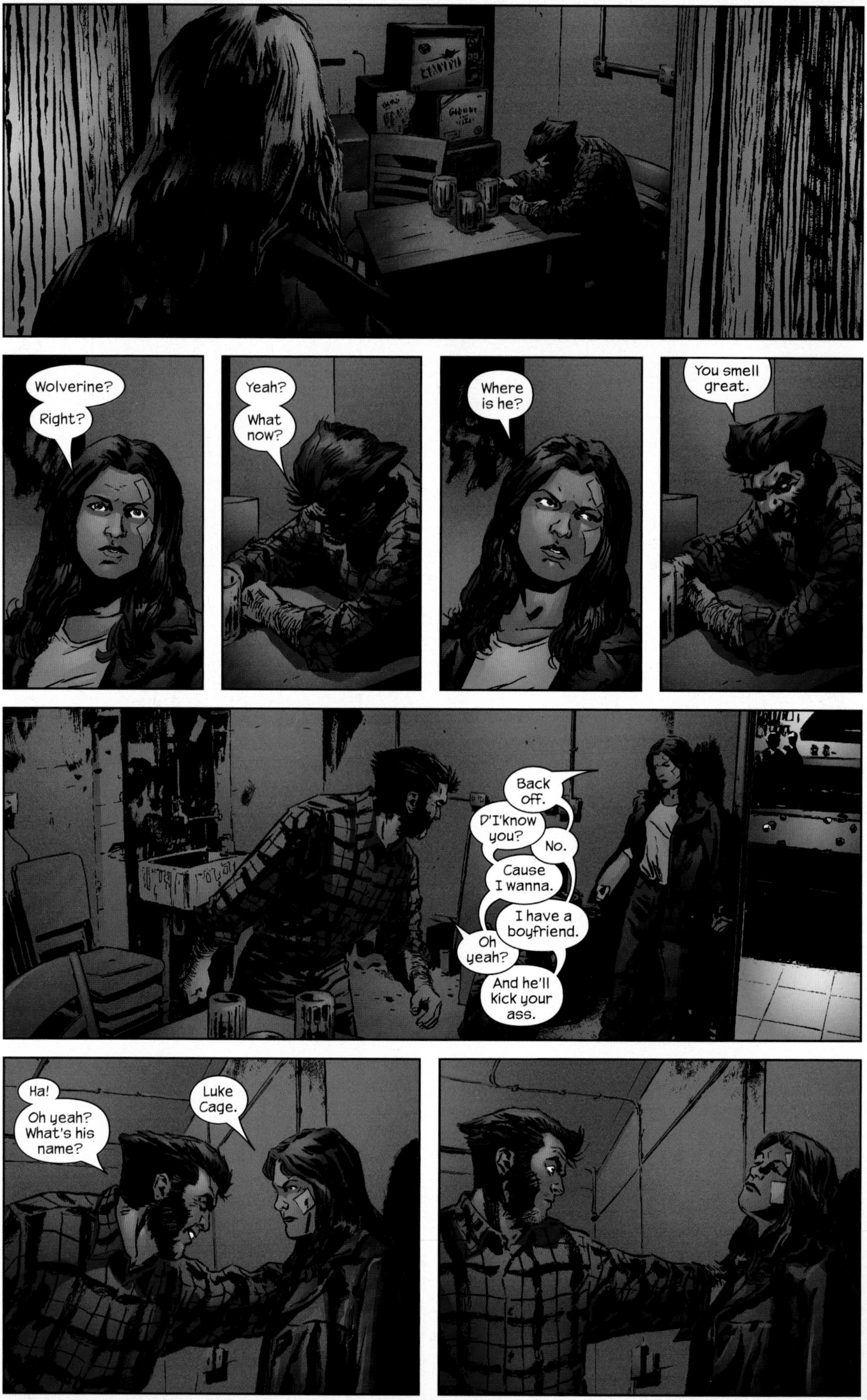
Wolverine?
Right?
Yeah?
What now?
Where is he?
You smell great.
Back off.
D'I'know you?
No.
Cause I wanna.
I have a boyfriend.
Oh yeah?
And he'll kick your ass.
Ha!
Oh yeah? What's his name?
Luke Cage.

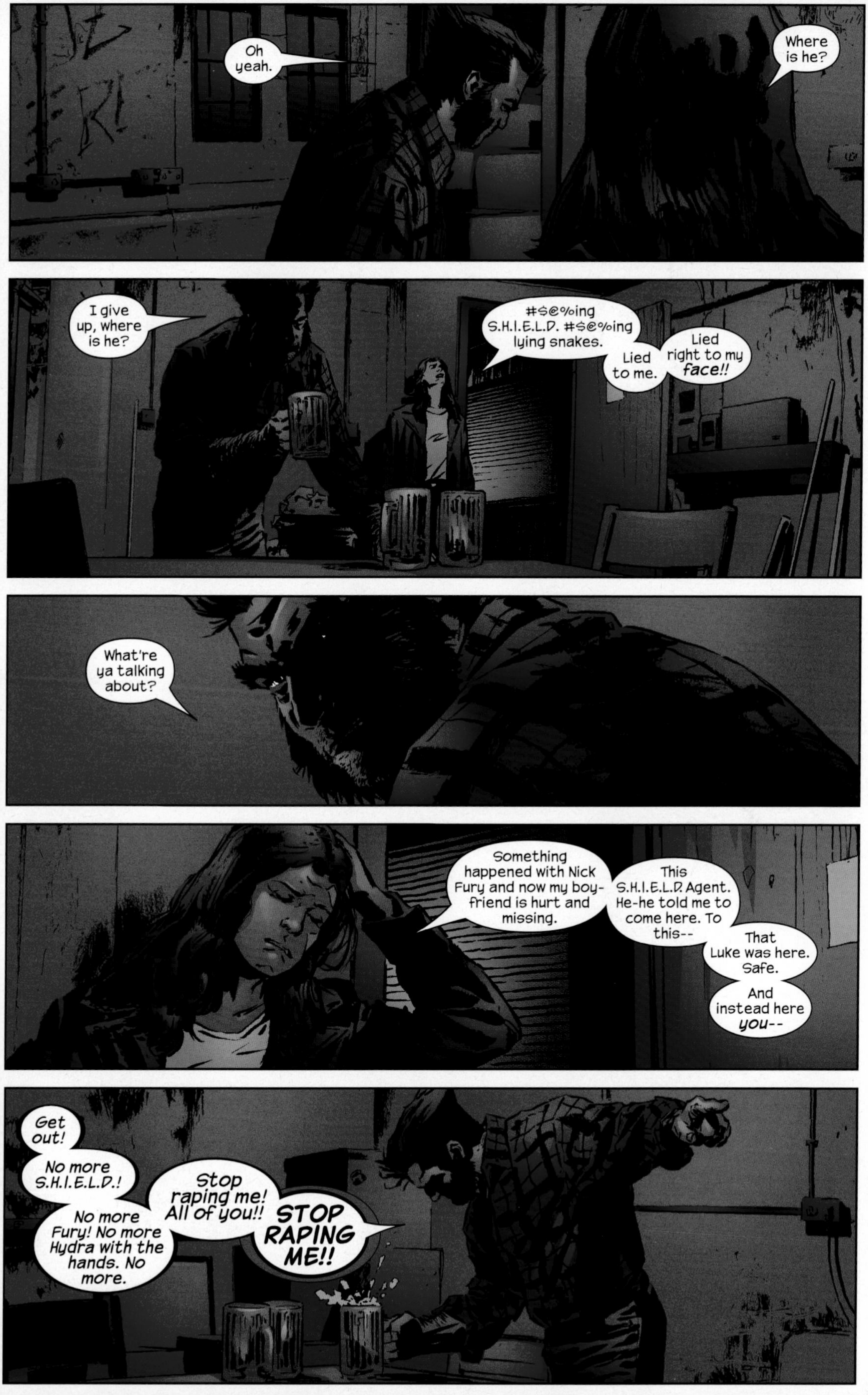
Oh yeah.
Where is he?
I give up, where is he?
#$@%ing S.H.I.E.L.D. #$@%ing lying snakes.
Lied to me.
Lied right to my *face!!*
What're ya talking about?
Something happened with Nick Fury and now my boy-friend is hurt and missing.
This S.H.I.E.L.D. Agent. He-he told me to come here. To this--
That Luke was here. Safe.
And instead here *you*--
Get out!
No more S.H.I.E.L.D.!
No more Fury! No more Hydra with the hands. No more.
Stop raping me! All of you!!
STOP RAPING ME!!

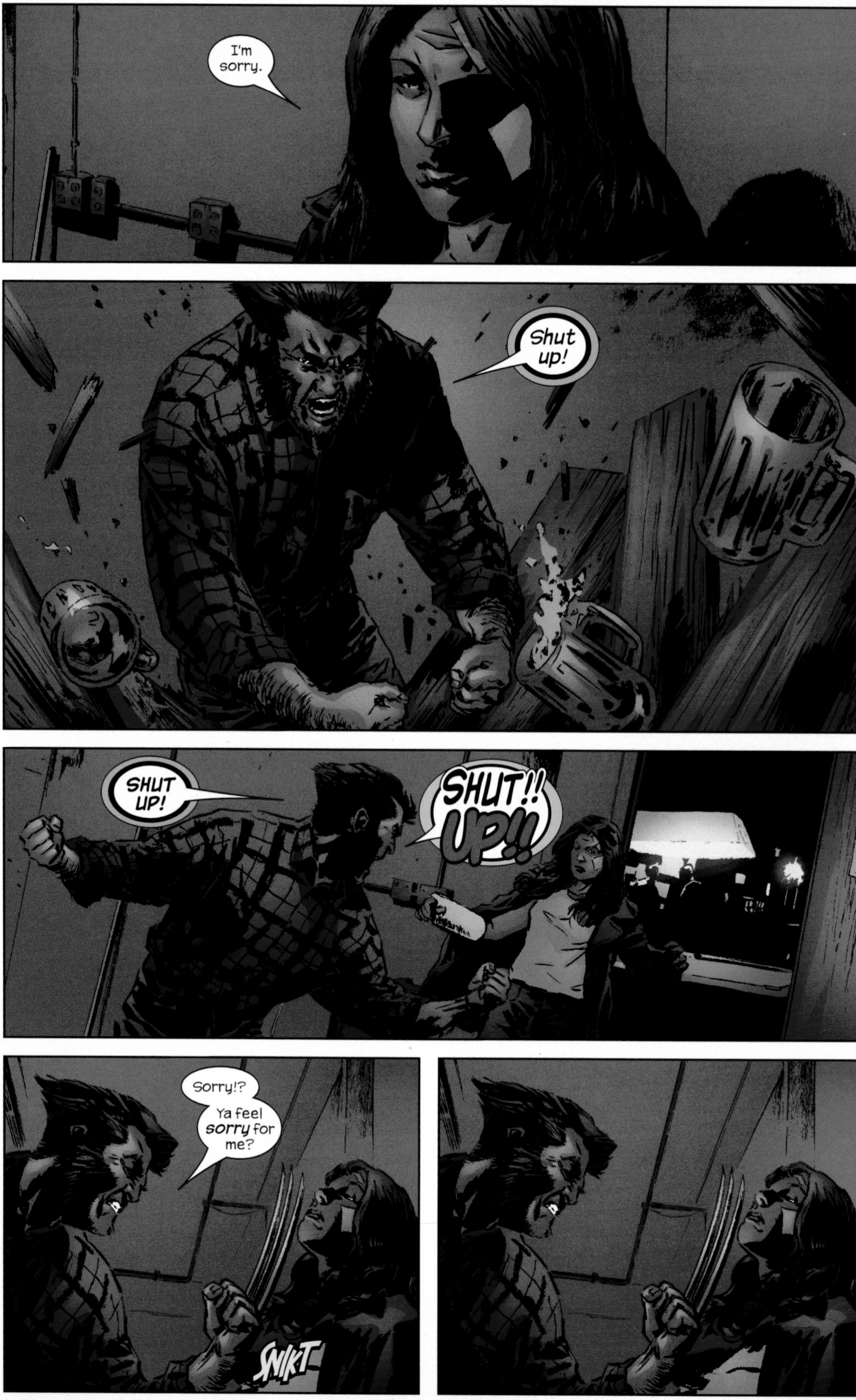
I'm sorry.
Shut up!
SHUT UP!
SHUT!! UP!!
Sorry!? Ya feel sorry for me?
SNIKT

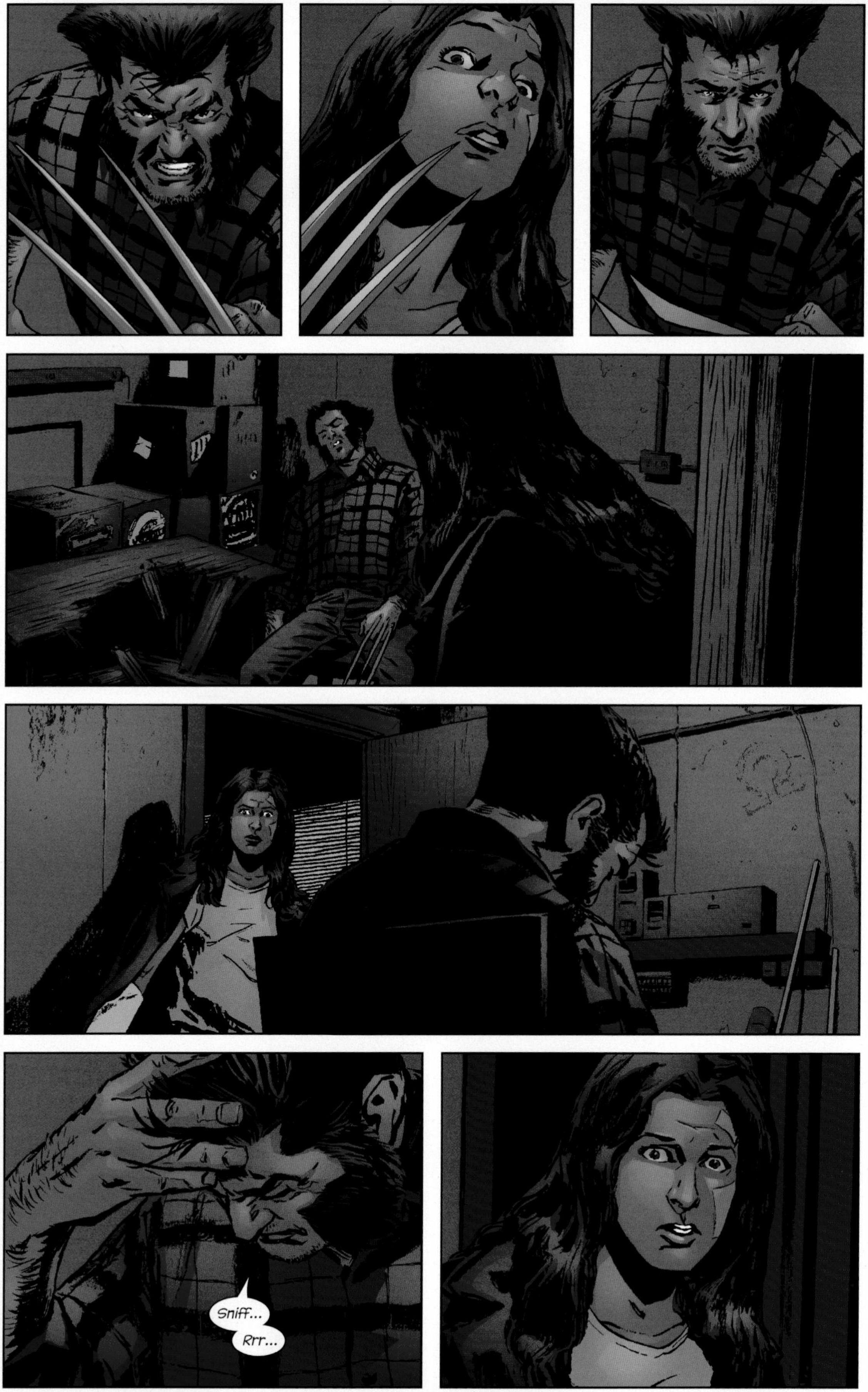
Sniff...
Rrr...

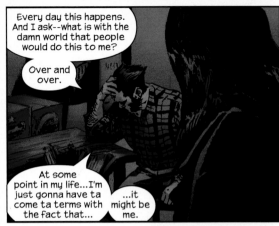

Every day of my life...
...my mind... or my body. There's no other word for it. They rape me.
Try ta get me to do somethin' I don't wanna do.

Every day this happens. And I ask--what is with the damn world that people would do this to me?
Over and over.
At some point in my life...I'm just gonna have ta come ta terms with the fact that...
...it might be me.

Know you can't tell from lookin' at me...
...but I'm usually not the self-pityin' type.

What is this? Why are we here?
I told you in the car-- that S.H.I.E.L.D. Agent has been trying to get me to throw Nick Fury under the bus. In print.
Screwing with me.
I don't KNOW why he sent us here.
Let's go.

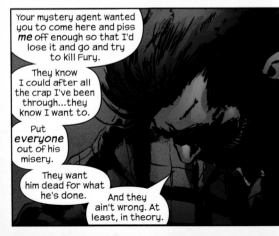

Your mystery agent wanted you to come here and piss me off enough so that I'd lose it and go and try to kill Fury.
They know I could after all the crap I've been through...they know I want to.
Put everyone out of his misery.
They want him dead for what he's done.
And they ain't wrong. At least, in theory.

What did he do?

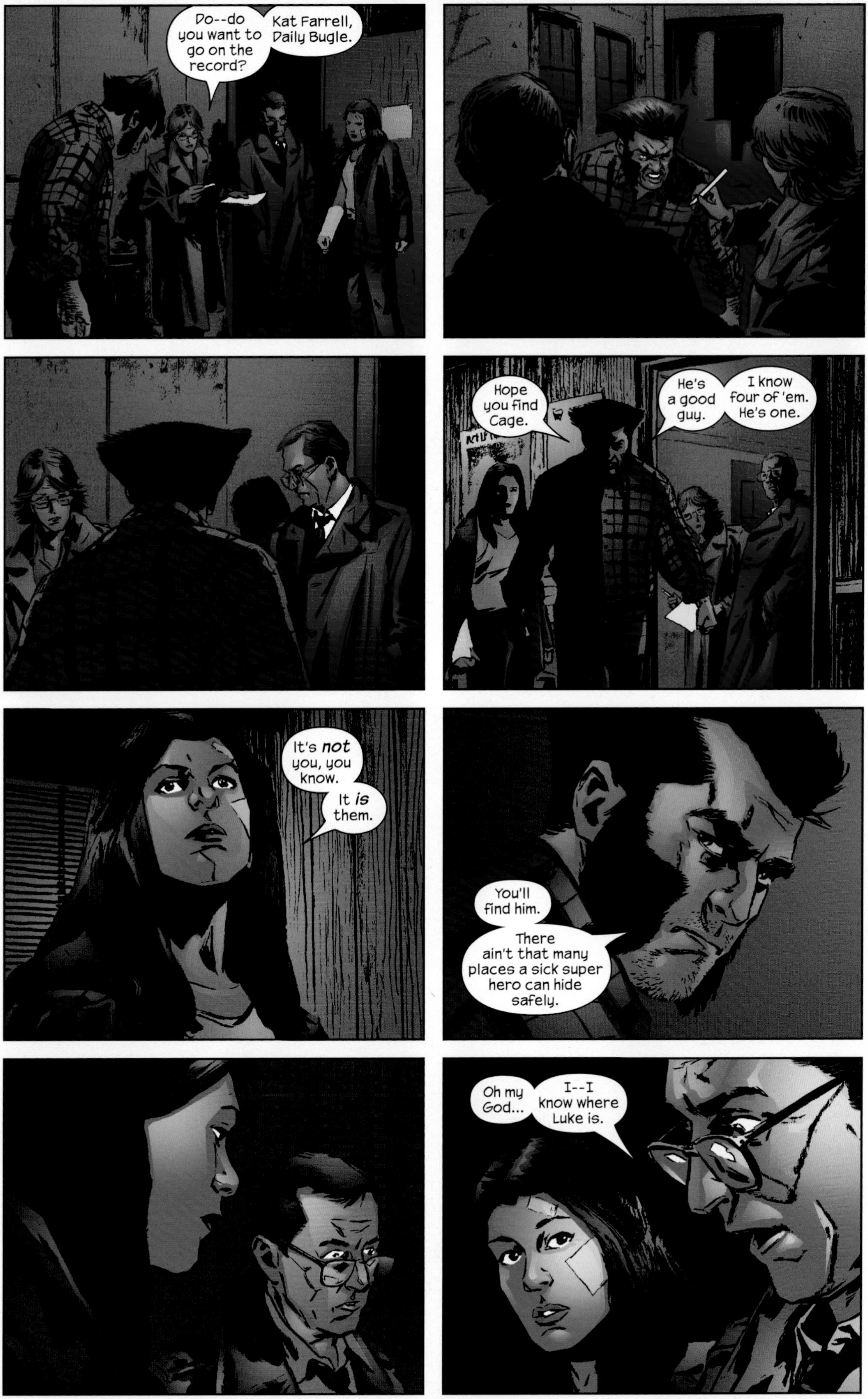
Do--do you want to go on the record?
Kat Farrell, Daily Bugle.
Hope you find Cage.
He's a good guy.
I know four of 'em. He's one.
It's *not* you, you know.
It *is* them.
You'll find him.
There ain't that many places a sick super hero can hide safely.
Oh my God...
I--I know where Luke is.

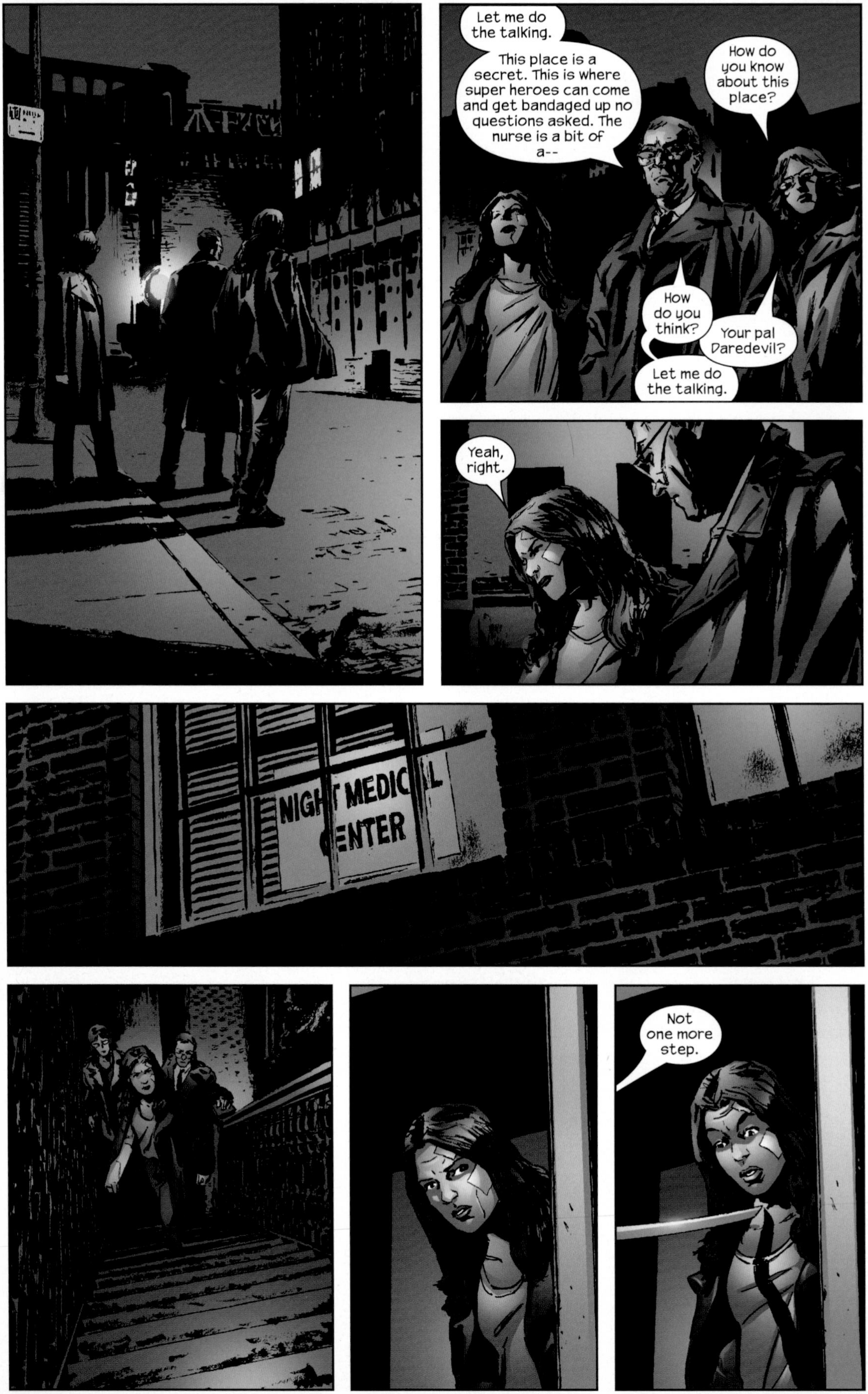
Let me do the talking.
This place is a secret. This is where super heroes can come and get bandaged up no questions asked. The nurse is a bit of a--
How do you know about this place?
How do you think?
Your pal Daredevil?
Let me do the talking.
Yeah, right.
NIGHT MEDIC L CENTER
Not one more step.

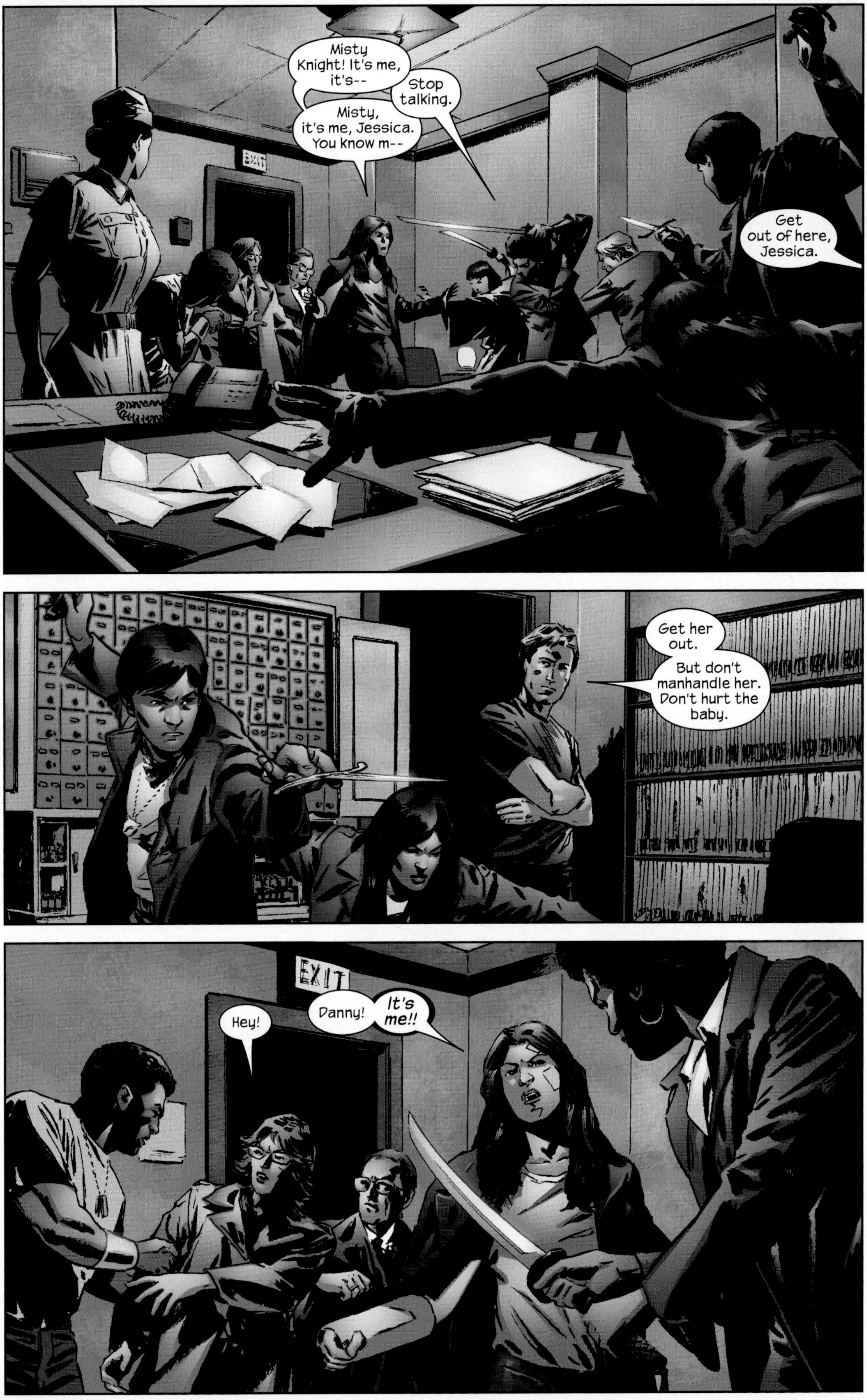
Misty Knight! It's me, it's--
Stop talking.
Misty, it's me, Jessica. You know m--
Get out of here, Jessica.
Get her out.
But don't manhandle her. Don't hurt the baby.
EXIT
Hey!
Danny!
It's me!!

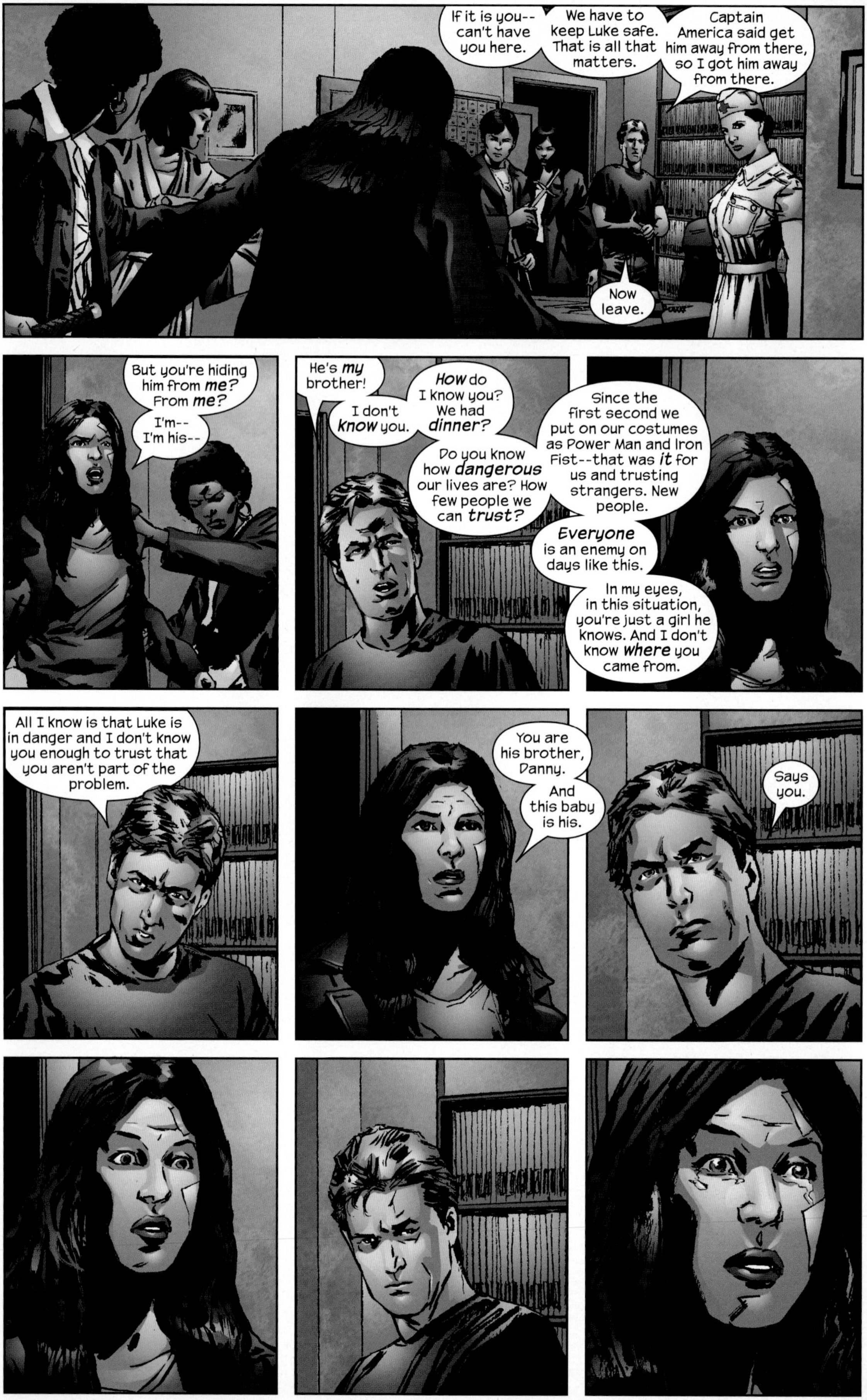

If it is you--
can't have you here.
We have to keep Luke safe. That is all that matters.
Captain America said get him away from there, so I got him away from there.
Now leave.
But you're hiding him from *me*? From *me*?
I'm--
I'm his--
He's *my* brother!
I don't *know* you.
How do I know you? We had *dinner*?
Do you know how *dangerous* our lives are? How few people we can *trust*?
Since the first second we put on our costumes as Power Man and Iron Fist--that was *it* for us and trusting strangers. New people.
Everyone is an enemy on days like this.
In my eyes, in this situation, you're just a girl he knows. And I don't know *where* you came from.
All I know is that Luke is in danger and I don't know you enough to trust that you aren't part of the problem.
You are his brother, Danny.
And this baby is his.
Says you.

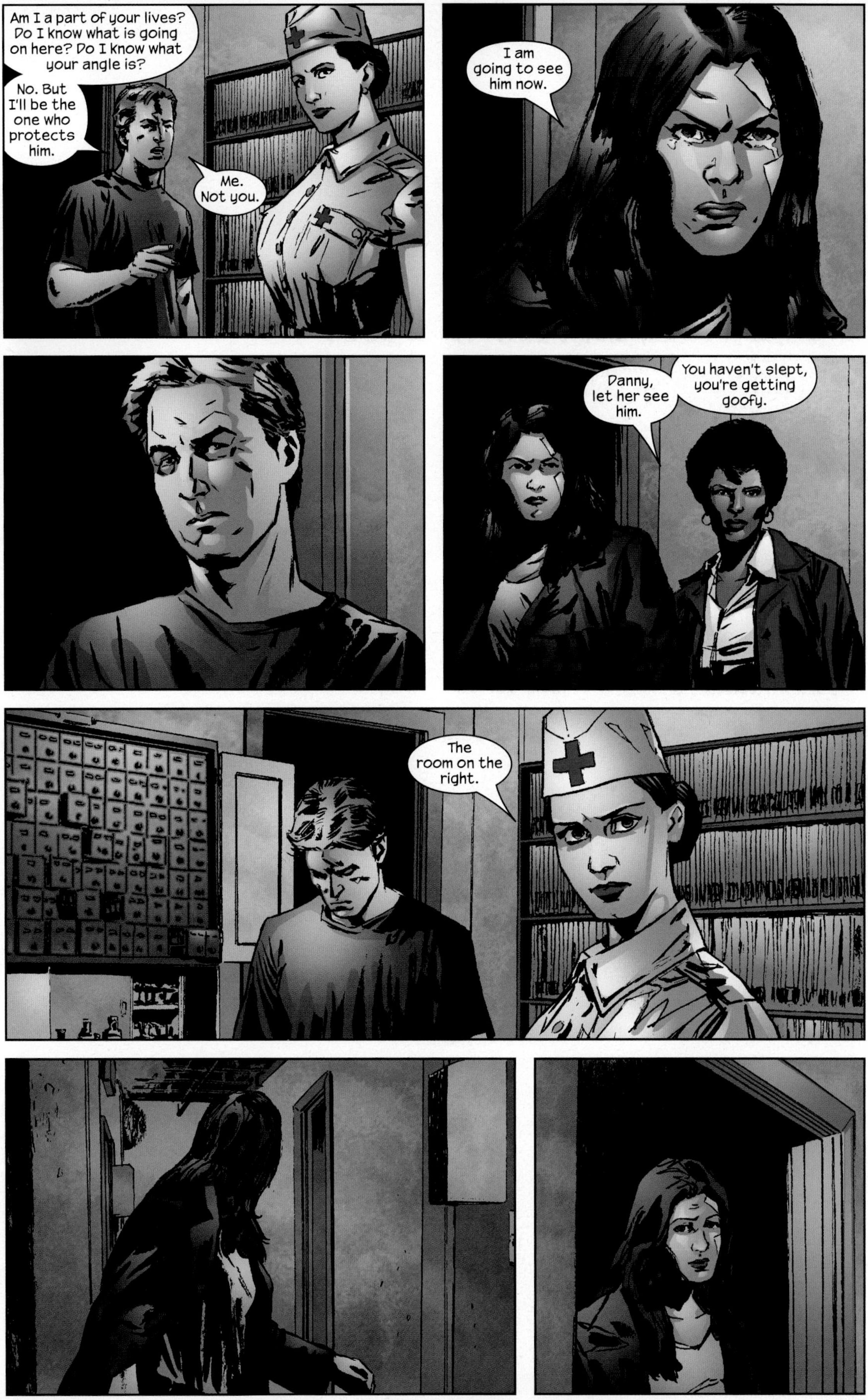
Am I a part of your lives? Do I know what is going on here? Do I know what your angle is?
No. But I'll be the one who protects him.
Me. Not you.
I am going to see him now.
Danny, let her see him.
You haven't slept, you're getting goofy.
The room on the right.

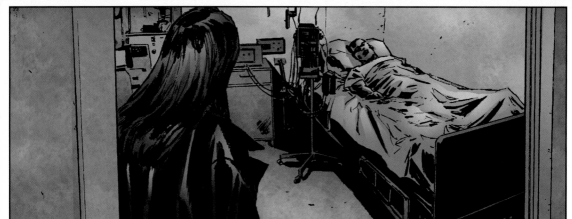

Hey...

Oh, thank God.

You okay?

Yes.

Baby?

She's in there.

That's all... ...that matters.

Hey... Didn't you used to be a tougher broad?

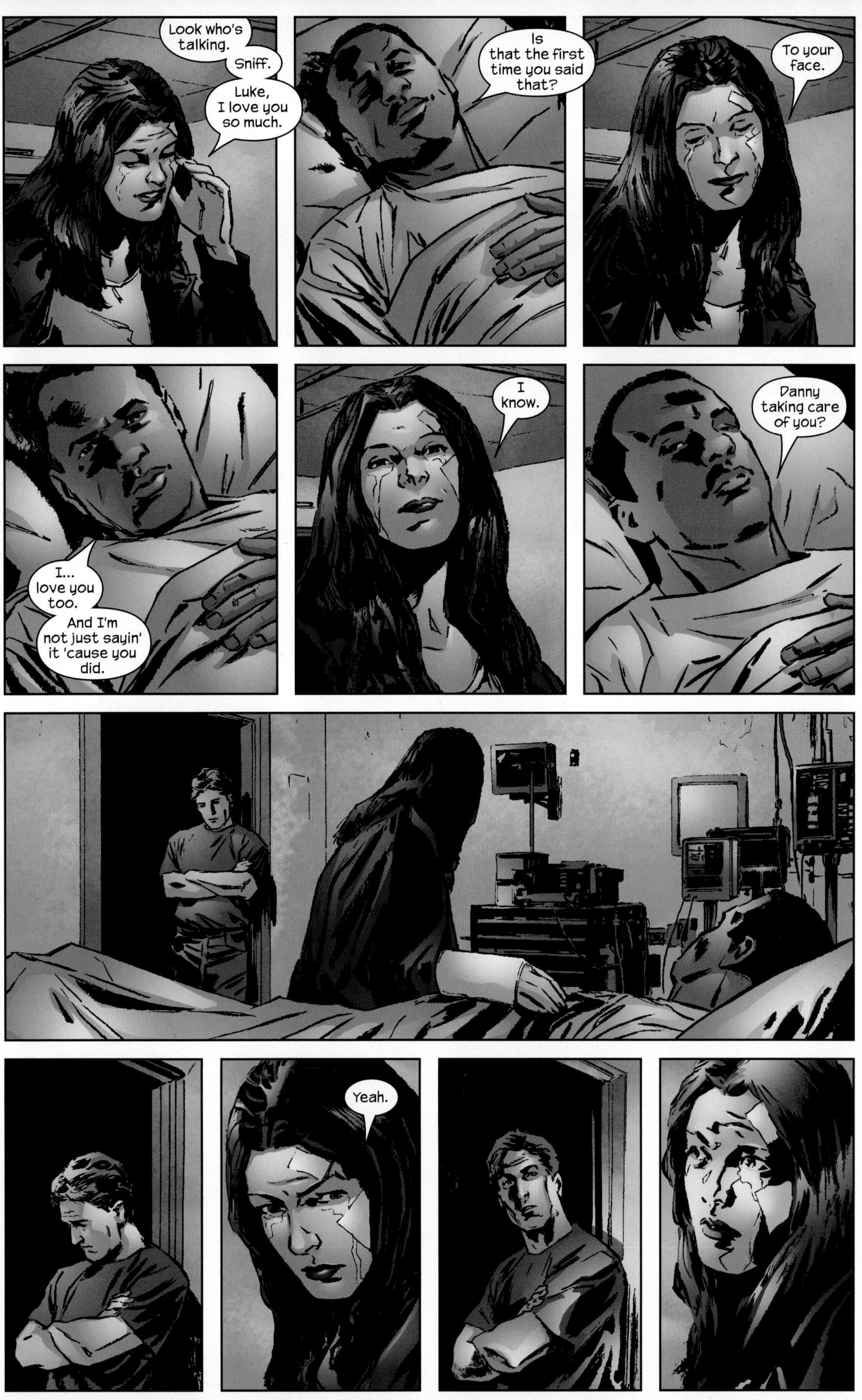
Look who's talking.
Sniff.
Luke, I love you so much.
Is that the first time you said that?
To your face.
I... love you too.
And I'm not just sayin' it 'cause you did.
I know.
Danny taking care of you?
Yeah.

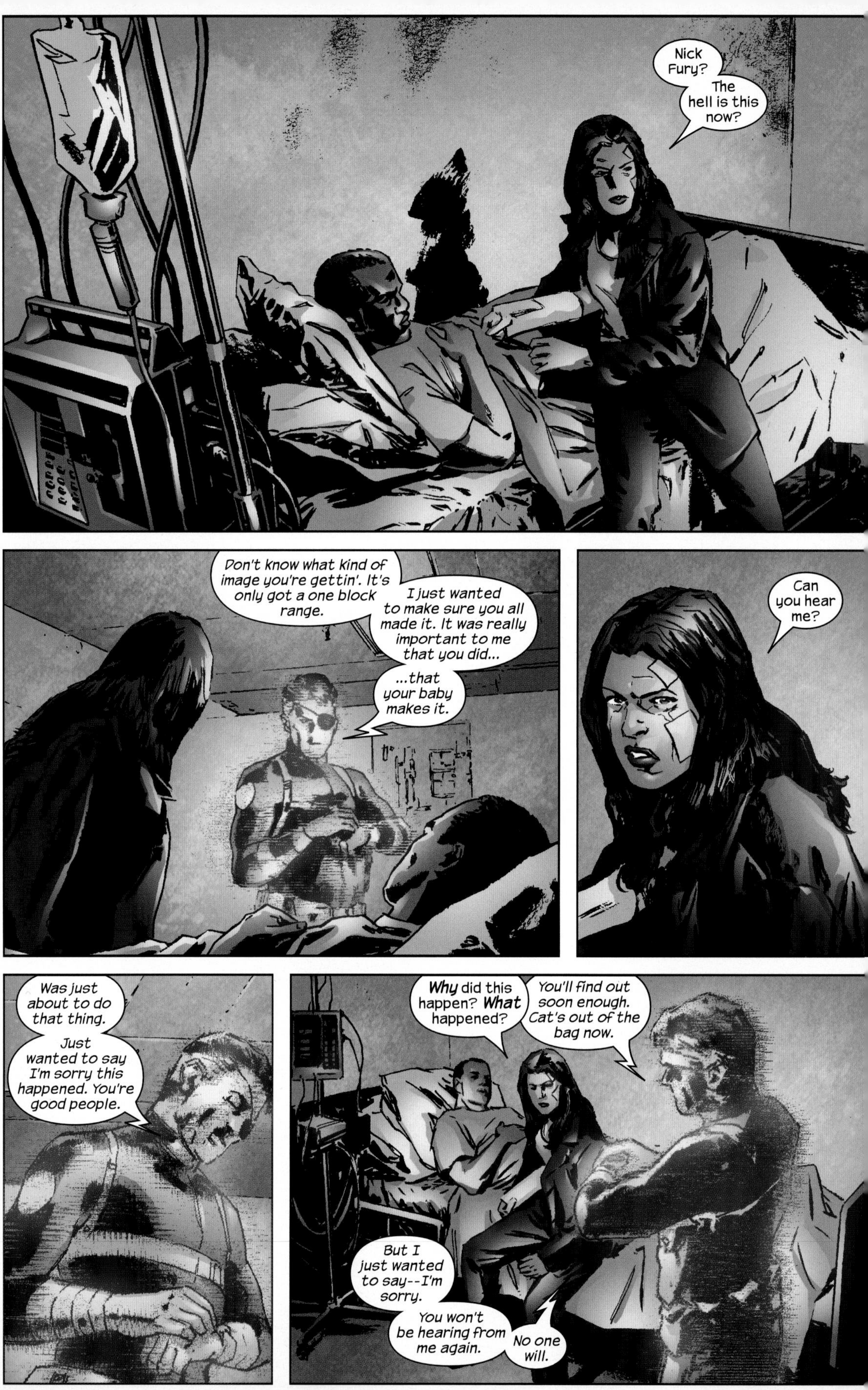
Nick Fury? The hell is this now?
Don't know what kind of image you're gettin'. It's only got a one block range.
I just wanted to make sure you all made it. It was really important to me that you did...
...that your baby makes it.
Can you hear me?
Was just about to do that thing.
Just wanted to say I'm sorry this happened. You're good people.
Why did this happen? What happened?
You'll find out soon enough. Cat's out of the bag now.
But I just wanted to say--I'm sorry.
You won't be hearing from me again.
No one will.

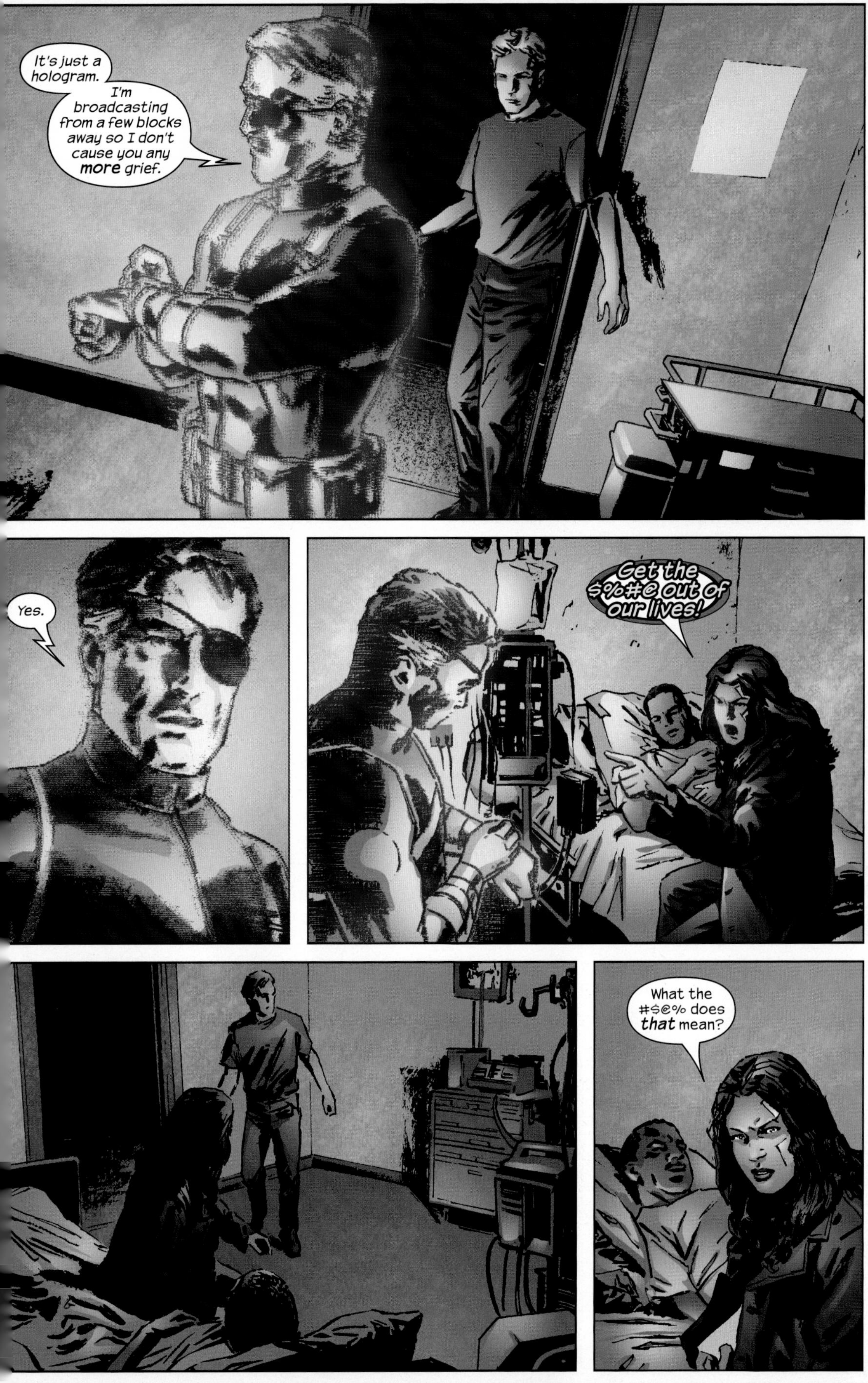
It's just a hologram.
I'm broadcasting from a few blocks away so I don't cause you any more grief.
Yes.
Get the $%#@ out of our lives!
What the #$@% does that mean?

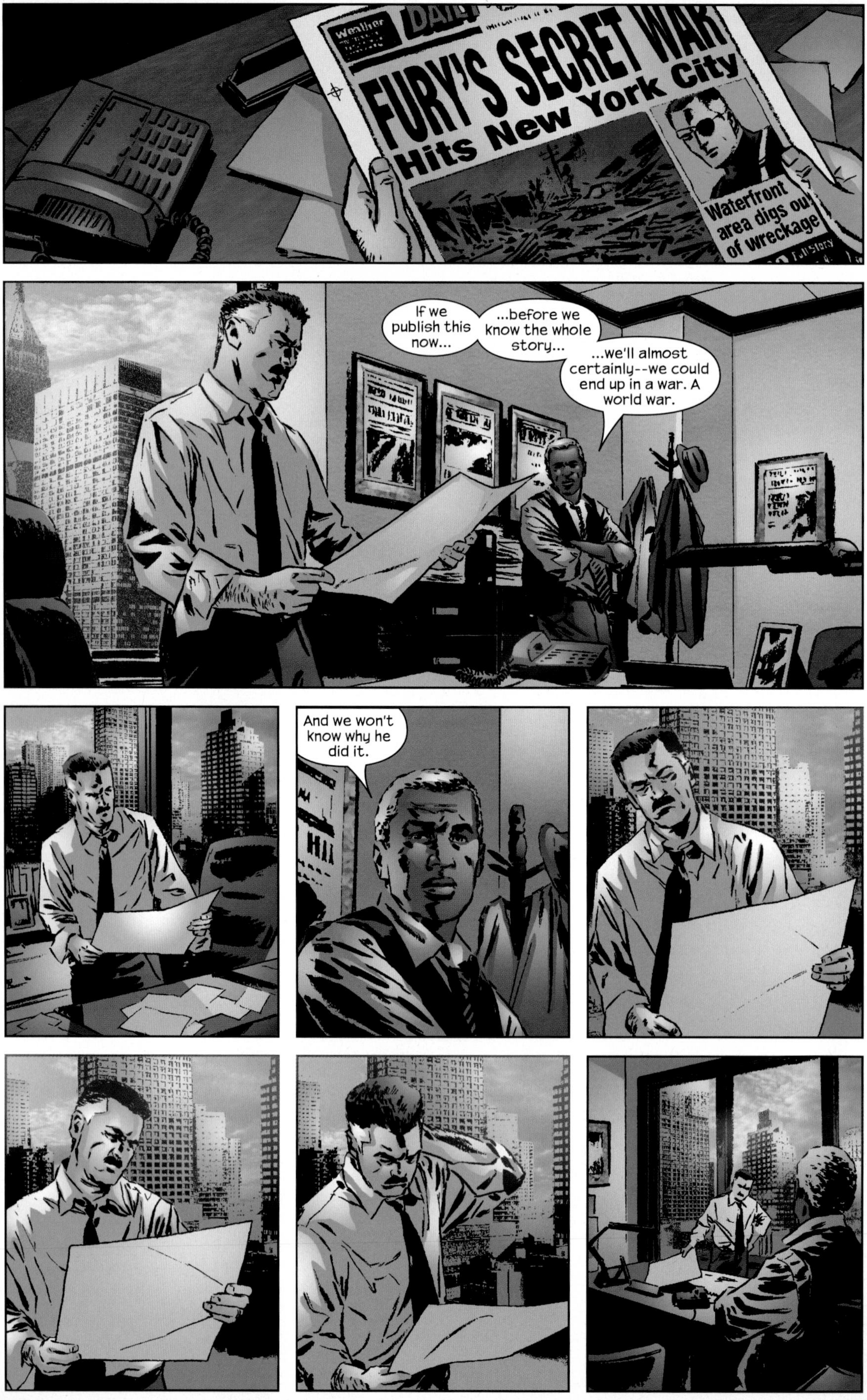

FURY'S SECRET WAR
Hits New York City
Waterfront area digs out of wreckage
If we publish this now...
...before we know the whole story...
...we'll almost certainly--we could end up in a war. A world war.
And we won't know why he did it.

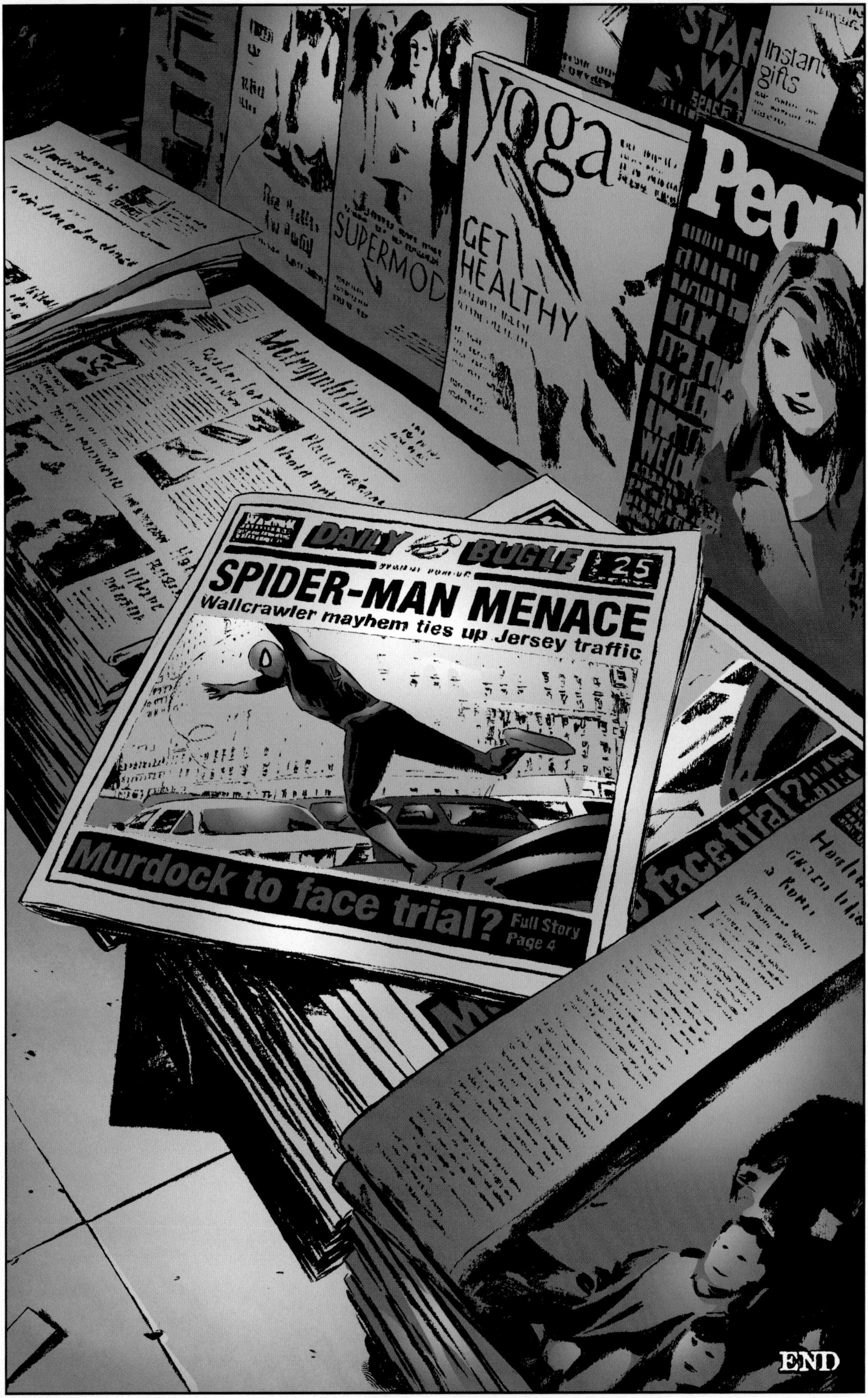

yoga
GET HEALTHY
SUPERMOD
Instant gifts
DAILY BUGLE
25
SPIDER-MAN MENACE
Wallcrawler mayhem ties up Jersey traffic
Murdock to face trial? Full Story Page 4
END

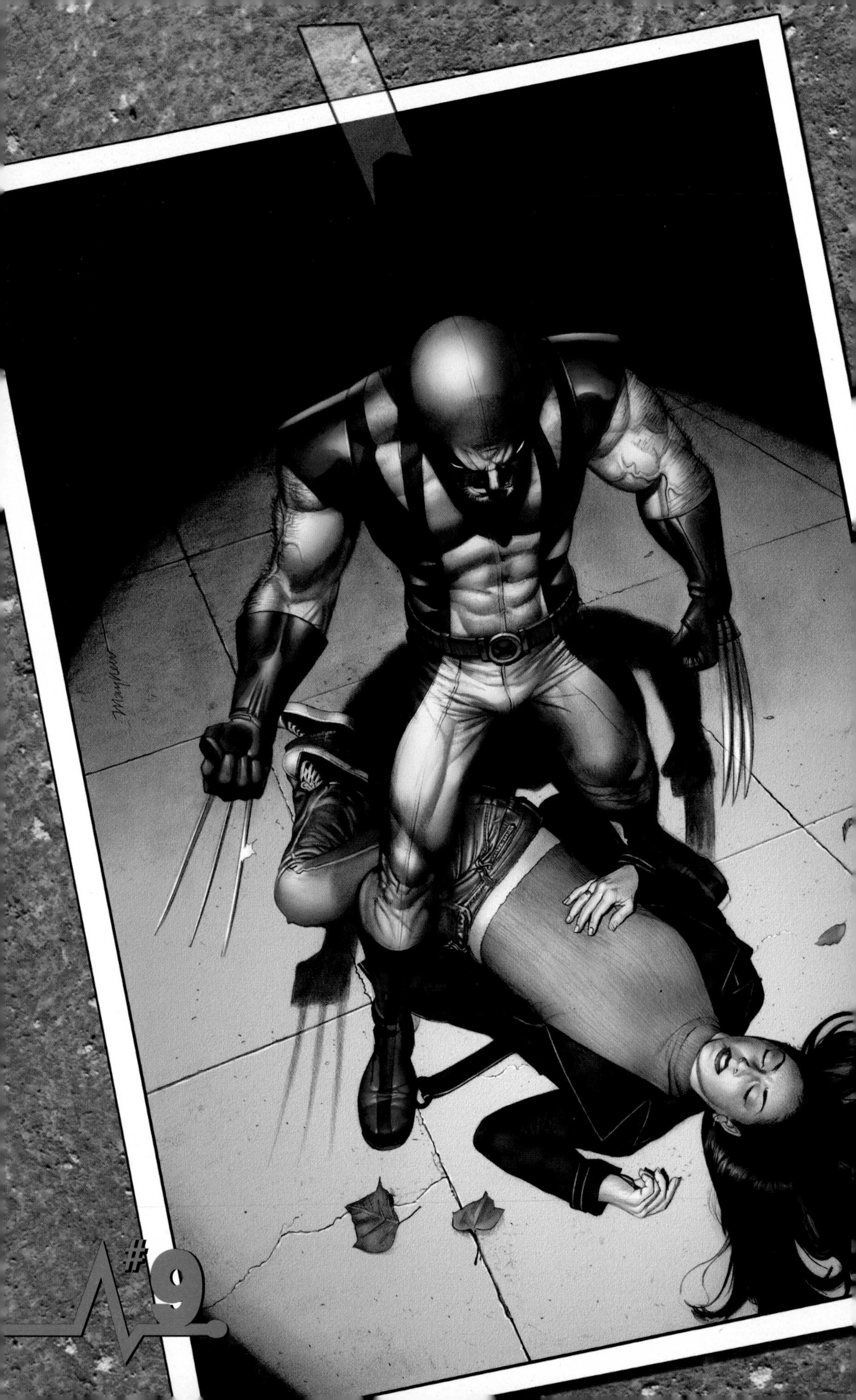
#9